MW00627459

"Bronwyn Jardin's memoir, *Light Through Broken Pieces*, is a compelling read. Her prose is lyrical and insightful, delivering not just wisdom from her own life, but observant snapshots of American culture in the 50's and 60's. I'm proud to call her one of my writing workshop graduates!"

LESLIE LEYLAND FIELDS, author of *Your Story Matters: Finding, Writing and Living the Truth of Your Life* and *The Wonder Years: 40 Women Over 40 on Aging, Faith, Beauty and Strength*

"Bronwyn Jardin is a remarkable storyteller. Her vivid detail and recall of events surrounding Hurricane Andrew in 1992 is astonishing and lands readers right smack in the middle of her tale. Illuminations in *Light Through Broken Pieces* also reveal Jardin's reflections and observations of weathering another kind of storm. Readers will relate to the emotional chaos she faced as a young girl, and the bravery needed to confront her fears with faith and grace."

JODY COLLINS, author of *Hearts on Pilgrimage, Poems & Prayers* and *Living in the Season Well-Reclaiming Christmas.*

"*Light Through Broken Pieces* is a beautifully written memoir of a storm-tossed life and a reminder that while we are shaped and formed by all kinds of terrifying weather, we are always seen and always loved."

CHRISTIE PURIFOY, Author of *Placemaker: Cultivating Places of Comfort, Beauty, and Peace;* and *Roots and Sky*

"With eloquence, honesty, and a steady pace, Bronwyn Best Jardin shares both personal tragedy and triumph of her life's story in her masterful style of prose. From her childhood home to her present place of personal peace, rooted in a deep Christian faith, Bronwyn presents a riveting and honest telling of both the pain and subsequent joys and peace she has weathered from childhood through adulthood–beginning and ending in hurricane-prone Florida. Bronwyn touches on universal themes that connect the reader in profound ways. *Light Through Broken Pieces* evokes and stirs a chorus of human emotions: love, loss, pain, trauma, fear and forgiveness among scores of others. Each line and page is shared in a richly told storytelling style and adept, often lyrical, prose. This is not just a tale of surviving one deadly hurricane, this is a story of looking back over a lifetime of personal storms, weathered well, with perseverance, grace and a faith that believes all things do work together for the good. This is a redemption story. A love story. This is a story to read and share. This is a story of Light. A light through the broken pieces is visible and palpable in the pages of this moving memoir."

ELIZABETH WYNNE MARSHALL, Poet, Artist, Host of Peabiddies Podcast

Light Through Broken Pieces

Christie,
Thank you for
joining me on this
journey!
Blessings,
Bronwyn

Light Through Broken Pieces

Bronwyn Best Jardin

SHELL-HOME BOOKS

LIGHT THROUGH BROKEN PIECES
Memoir of a Storm Survivor

Shell-Home Books

Copyright © 2021 by Bronwyn Best Jardin

ISBN 978-1-7371116-0-3

Printed in the United States of America

ALL RIGHTS RESERVED.

No portion of this book may be reproduced, stored in a retrieval system, or transmitted in any form or by any means mechanical, electronic, scanning, photocopy, recording or other except for brief quotations in critical reviews or articles without prior written concent from the author.

Scripture quotations, unless otherwise noted, all are from The Holy Bible, English Standard Version(ESV)®, copyright©2001 by Crossway, a publishing ministry of Good News Publishers. Used by permission. All rights reserved. The "ESV" and "English Standard Version" are registered trademarks of Crossway. Use of either trademark requires permission of Crossway.

Scripture quotations marked NKJV are taken from the New King James Version®. ©1982 by Thomas Nelson. Used by permission. All rights reserved.

The content in this book is based upon true events as recalled by the author. Some names have been changed to protect privacy. Some incidents are composites of real situations and any resemblance to people living or dead is purely coincidental.

Published in the United States by Shell-Home Books, LLC, Lithia, FL
P.O. Box 185, Lithia, FL 33547

www.bronwynbestjardin.com

Cover design by Kris Camealy/ Cover art by Ralph "Rafa" Lopez, from photo by Julia Joppien/Unsplash
Back cover photo by Emily Martin

Contents

LIGHT THROUGH BROKEN PIECES

LIGHT THROUGH BROKEN PIECES

Memoir of a Storm Survivor

Bronwyn Best Jardin

Faith is the strength by which a shattered world shall emerge into the light.
Helen Keller

For my beloved grandchildren: Luke, Samuel, Abigail, Phoebe, Micaiah, Solomon, and Boaz. The meaning of this story will grow as you do.

With Gratitude

What a blessing to have crossed paths with so many generous and talented people in this life! To all my family and friends who have listened to bits and pieces herein and encouraged me through this long project, thank you for so much for your love and support.

Stephanie Polzin, wherever you are, thank you for recommending me to the *Northern Virginia Writing Project* Summer Institute at George Mason University. The intensive course was the ignition switch, and this engine was off and running. I was a mere long-term sub teacher, but you had faith in my potential, and surely, you had a hand in the gift of a full-time position in one of the best schools of my career.

Dr. Don Gallehr, I still remember you and the late Victor Kryston running the *Project's* Summer Institute. My disaster story was fresh and raw. Thank you for providing a nurturing environment, not only for workshopping early drafts, but also for a professional growth experience with other educators unlike any I have experienced since.

Leslie Leyland Fields and the women of the 2017 New Smyrna Beach Non-Fiction Writing workshop, you pre-read, you listened, you encouraged. "Yes," you told me. "Write this book." I will be forever grateful to you all.

Women of *Refine, the Retreat* '18, '19, and '21: If I try to name you all, I will leave someone out, so, to all of you, few joys in life compare to the fellowship and friendship nurtured in The Pines. Most of all, sisters in Spirit, you are inspiring!

To all those who helped launch this book, I am so

honored that you wanted to help! Thank you for sharing the news with your circle of friends. What a blessing you all are!

Sarah Hazen, you looked at early drafts and called it as you saw it, and I love that about you. You cast a line when I drift too far from the shore. I have always trusted your honesty.

Pam Lehman, once again, you let me steal some of your summer vacation time. Then, you offered helpful and heartfelt feedback. I am so grateful to you.

Jody Collins, I know you were a great classroom teacher! I so appreciate the generous gift of your time and skills as a part of the editorial team. Thank you, Linda Chivington, Leslie L. Fields, Teressa Mahoney, Elizabeth Wynne Marshall, and Christie Purifoy, for the generous offering of your time and feedback on my story. You are gifted women I truly admire.

Christen Ditchfield, you are an editor extraordinaire. For all the extra time you put into the job, I will always be grateful. And I will not forget your suggestion for the *next* book. . . if I live that long! Abundant thanks for guiding the way back when I wandered.

Carol, you know this story. Thank you, Sis, for reassurance when I worried about handling the hard stuff with care. I'm so glad after my sketchy start as your bratty little sister, we grew to be friends. Love you more than I love my computer backpack. Way more.

Ralph *Rafa* Lopez, your rendering of the beautiful photo by Julie Joppien is just perfect. Thank you for once again sharing your watercolor gift with all of us. Love you, brother.

Seana, Kris, and James, you and your families are treasure I never deserved. How sweet are your offerings of love and encouragement (along with some juicy tidbits), as I write. You make me one very proud "Momma-mmm." Truly, I love you all.

Kris, as a fellow author, you still lead the way for your old Mom. For all the phone calls, mini-tutorials, free advice, and hands-on assistance, I will always hold dear the time you spend helping me. Thank you, sweetheart.

Roy, I love that, in many ways, this is your story too. Hasn't this project's "pregnancy" been the longest? You have listened, read, evaluated, given me space and time to nurture this baby. Congratulations "Dad!" At least you won't have to teach this one to drive or send it to college. Love you most, book Papa. Cue our *kealoha* island music: "Only You, only you. . .You and I."

Most of all, thank You, Lord Jesus! As one of your lambs who often has found herself bumbling into the brambles, or worse, stubbornly choosing the wrong way, I sing praise for you my Shepherd, Redeemer of my soul. Indeed, you are my All in All, my Eternal Light; any glory in this project goes to You!

A Note About the Book

Dear Reader,

You may notice as I amble back and forth across time that my train of thought moves between decades and dates, time and place.

Each chapter is headed with the particulars of the setting—sometimes the neighborhood, sometimes the State, sometimes the time of day or the date on the calendar. Some entries, such as the event of Hurricane Andrew, are simply identified with the date.

Keep this in mind as my stream-of-consciousness retelling of this story unfolds. I pray as we journey together, you will gather from my words not only what happened because of a hurricane, but how I have weathered the storms of my life.

Yours,
Bronwyn

Prologue

We are all broken. That's how the light gets in.

Attributed to Ernest Hemingway

On August 24, 1992, my home was ripped apart and my town blew away. Under mandatory Homestead Air Force Base evacuation orders, we sheltered with my parents in the South Miami home of my youth. In total darkness, wind alternately thundered, howled, and shrieked like an invading army of demons loosed from the depths. The wall behind my back shuddered and I cradled my sleeping son on my lap for a six hour eternity. As a child, I, too, had once slept through hurricanes. But on that night, bathed in sweat in the sealed house, my heart pounding so hard, it hurt, I feared the old home was going to crack open. My imagination clicked back and forth like changing television channels: the fate of our base house versus my parents' forty-year-old rancher. Would both structures stand through the storm? Would we all survive in a closet if the roof ripped away?

Some of you are old enough to remember the live television report the next morning, a startling moment as you picked up your coffee or poured cereal for the kids. Maybe you were young enough to be starting a new school year. Perhaps you saw the caption, "Hurricane Andrew devastates Homestead, Florida," and said, "Oh, wow! Look

1

at that!" And then, as most of us do, you went on with your summer day. Unless you have lived through one, a natural disaster is an odorless, flavorless, two-dimensional sound bite in your climate-controlled living room or den.

Several miles south of Miami, in the immediate wake of catastrophe, that day began with shocked survivors crawling from their bathrooms and out from under mattresses, collapsed walls, and roof trusses. Some victims died fleeing too late the astonishing crush of nature. A few even began celebrating the night before, throwing a "hurricane party." Search and rescue dogs helped recover the revelers a day or two later, their bodies tangled in wreckage and beer cans.

Desperate homeowners graffitied their own houses. Scrawled telegrams went out to all the world in white latex on broken brown roofs, black spray on stucco walls:

Help us!
Andrew-1, Homestead-0
Stay Strong, God bless
We will Rebuild!

Two hundred and fifty thousand people were suddenly homeless. Among them was a community of six and half thousand at Homestead Air Force Base. I am one of those thousands.

The base house I shared with my husband and three children was not ours, but we had made it home. Military families do that; arrive with their furniture, all bearing scars of repeated moving and storage, and proceed to dress a naked four-bedroom dwelling with new blinds and curtains in comforting colors. Familiar books, travel memorabilia, and toys, along with a hallway of framed certificates, plaques, and family photos–generations of brides, babies, and graduates–create a warm and welcoming abode. Had we been allowed to paint an S.O.S on our roof, my cry would have been "Where now, Lord?"

Two houses met different fates during the hurricane's assault. But my story is not a recycling of media features about a mostly forgotten headline. You can find colorful books about the storm, with plenty of breathtaking scenes of devastation and heartbroken victims. For many years, the media called Andrew "The Big One." To my surprise, this One blew me back to taking a second look at a life, long tossed by gales, mostly unseen behind the walls of my childhood. This is a story of surviving, of longing for love, of unlocking faith and trust from a hurting heart, closed and guarded like a buried safe deposit box.

One dark endless night, I lost a home. Thousands of nights later, long after salvaging, our bits and pieces and relics lost their importance. I have found treasure greater than anything this earth can hold. I was spared to tell you about the light now illuminating the broken pieces of this story.

Child of Storms

Smooth seas do not make skillful sailors.

-African proverb

In the dark before dawn, on August 24, 1992, a monster named Andrew came for our family. When the Category 5 hurricane roared across the southern tip of the Florida peninsula, shredding our community and the towns of Homestead and Florida City, I can't say we weren't physically ready. But even as a native of the Sunshine State, I could not imagine the ferocity of a storm that would forever change building codes and restructure the lives of survivors. My life's course was so altered by Hurricane Andrew, it has taken years to fully discover the storm's imprint on the person I am today.

I was a Florida child, born in hurricane season, a foretelling of my life on several levels. The 1953 Atlantic season was the first time an organized list of female names was used to designate the region's storms.[1] Although my sister's name, "Carol," made the premier cut, a Celtic name like "Bronwyn" was hardly acceptable in my extended family, much less recognized by the National Weather Service or any non-British person in the United States. Also, it was possibly a miracle I arrived in late summer that year.

In some random slip of the tongue, my mother once informed me that after a miserable pregnancy carrying my sister, she didn't think she was going to have any more children. Overwhelmed by nausea, weak and bedridden for the duration, she endured my father learning how to daily poke a needleful of vitamin shots into her behind. I can't say I blame her for her revulsion to throwing up everything she tried to eat for most of a year. She may have been one of the unfortunate women that spend *all* nine months suffering from hyperemesis. One course of that ongoing misery would have made me a volunteer for tubal ligation! Our daughter Seana would have never grown up fighting her sibs, Kris and James, for the last piece of chocolate cream pie.

Knowing my poor mother's story, I have since imagined the following scenario: I began my nine-month fetal journey at the outset of the festive holiday season of 1952. However, by Valentine's Day, also Mom's birthday, she no doubt found a sudden aversion to her favorite heart-shaped box of Russell Stover chocolates, while my tiny heart was ticking away inside her. From her perspective, I must have been a twitching little time-bomb.

My hospital birth was not memorable for her, perhaps because in the fifties, laboring mothers were injected with a drug cocktail of morphine and scopolamine, named "Twilight Sleep." Although she would not remember pain, the unconscious woman, often in restraints, thrashed and moaned, while her obstetrician prepped for the delivery. Using long forceps, resembling a metal pair of foot-long salad tongs, the doctor would pull babies down from the womb. A groggy mom awoke, often disoriented, confused, even given to hallucinations, to find a nurse presenting her with a neatly swaddled, and in some cases, woozy, infant.[2] Truly a miracle of modern medicine that countless moms and post-World War II babies survived!

My father, excluded from the delivery room in those

ancient days, recounted several times in my life, that the doctor found him in the "Waiting Room," and announced: "You have a beautiful, healthy daughter, kissed by dimples all over her face." My mother certainly had cause for celebration after her recovery: no more long weeks of feeling half-dead while giving me life. Now, she had a new, robust baby with a name no one else could pronounce or spell.

Carol was a Christmas baby of the forties, so naming her was easy. But Mom, an avid reader, had always liked the name "Bronwen" (Bronwyn) from *How Green Was My Valley*, a novel about Welsh coal miners. The Waco, Texas, relatives, Dad's people, said "Wh-u-ut?!" when she suggested the name for my sister. "Miss Preggie" put up with their protests with the firstborn, but with her second daughter, and LAST child, she deserved to have it her way. Dad, no doubt, capitulated because he admired beautiful Irish actress, Maureen O'Hara, star of the film version of the novel.

During our annual August trek to hot-as-Hades central Texas, my paternal grandfather, Eugene Best, my "Bapoo," true to his reserved British roots, puffed contentedly on our gift of new pipe tobacco and refused to call me by my name. He nicknamed me "Babs," as my initials were B.A.B. Dad's second-generation German mother, Sadie, called "Mamoo," loved on me with her great soft arms sweeping like porch swings and made doll clothes and angel food cake for my birthday; but she, too, struggled with her youngest grandchild's name, calling me something resembling, "Brahmin."

Dad often called me "Bron," which sounded a bit masculine, and I did grow up the tomboy of the family. When I wasn't hanging like a chimpanzee from the branches of a ficus or mango tree with the neighborhood boys my age, I learned how to throw a softball and sit alongside my father as he taught me the finer nuances of Baylor (*Sic'em, Bears!*) football on Saturday afternoon TV. My sister, possibly miffed at losing "only child" status, lovingly called me "Birdbrain" for most of my single-digit years.

§§§

Hurricanes played a principal role in our family drama from the start. My parents were supposed to get married on September 15, 1945, but they didn't. Friends and family were gathered in Miami, Florida, Mom's hometown, for their "big day," and it didn't happen. They didn't have any electricity!

South Florida had just been ravaged by a Category 4 unnamed storm, known in the books as the "Homestead Hurricane." In today's dollars, its 143 mph winds wreaked fifty million dollars in damage, mostly destroying the small town of Homestead[3]. My folks did, of course, get married—two days later than planned. Most of Miami had no electricity, leaving dark the interior of their church. Under heavy skies still visible in the old black and white photographs, in a glow of candles and lantern light, they celebrated their wedding with guests seated on folding lawn chairs.

That my parents married while storm clouds were still scuttling off Florida's shores, leaves me to wonder at God's sense of irony. Literally, tropical storms were endemic to the Sunshine State. Figuratively, I would spend many years of my youth longing for calmer winds and clearer skies. Carol, seven years my senior, and I, often wonder how our parents, with such incompatible personality types, ever felt an attraction. Theirs was a war-time romance. Love and war always pulse with urgency, and it was no different for Mom and Dad.

In 1941, Arthur (Art) Best, a graduate of Baylor University Business School in his home of Waco, Texas, was a young station manager for a fledgling international airline, Pan American Airways. Sent from Brownsville to Caracas, Venezuela, in 1945, because of his Spanish language skills, he was destined to meet there a petite Irish-French beauty, Elizabeth Tucker, an interior designer sent from Miami's Moore's Furniture Store.

Someone had nicknamed her "Taffy," which invites all kinds of speculation. Sweet as candy? Sticky in an argument? Maybe "Taffy Tucker " just tripped off the tongue. Fresh from Parsons Design School in New York, she was on assignment to decorate Pan American's terminal at the Caracas Airport. She loved to dance, design furnished rooms, and read mystery and history. At that moment, embarking on her new career, she needed to snap a photo of the terminal. There was a problem. She asked for someone to get a pilot to please move one of Pan American's DC-3's to another parking space. It was blocking her line-of-sight. "Audacious," the ground crew must have thought. But this little doll (as they called them then) was sticking to her assignment and wasn't taking no for an answer. As the story goes, someone pointed to the tall, big boned "drink of water" across the tarmac: Art Best was the man to get it done. Probably the most fun he'd had in airport management yet! I still wonder if a promise of a dinner-dance date sealed the deal.

The second World War was about to end, and a celebratory mood hung over the Americans in South America like a room full of piñatas. My father shared a house with several other American bachelors and was the "designated driver" of the posse. The guys with dates frequently socialized with card games or beach trips.

In my father's journals, he wrote that he almost "blew

it," after meeting Miss Taffy. She and a girlfriend stopped by to see the housemates on the way to the beach. Deep in some serious poker, Dad looked up, said, "Hi!" and went back to considering how much to bet on what looked like a "straight flush." Good thing he beat the odds. The Miami girl gave him a second chance. After a mere three months and a few outings to dinner-dances, movies, and the beach, Dad decided she was "the one." Due to job-related conflicts, he had to send her engagement ring to Miami via a fellow bachelor. Perhaps a bit underwhelming?

Of course, my mother, as bride-to-be, introduced Art to the Florida family. His gregarious, cheery personality, which no doubt had opened many a gateway for him, swung wide the screened door on my mother's Miami home. Her father, Hastin, a tall, flinty-eyed, stiff man whom I would one day call "Grandy," liked him immediately. My "Mamaa," Belle, wheelchair-bound from polio since her thirties, accepted her daughter's decision to marry and her future son-in-law with less bitterness than when my mother left home for school in New York.

Back then, Mamaa had protested by burning all my mother's scrapbooks and photo albums. Even as Mom shared this with me after more than two decades, her quavering voice betrayed her shattered heart. All the pictures of her high school friends were destroyed. It was hard for me to imagine a mother being so cruel. I don't know if my grandmother experienced any joy of living after losing her ability to walk while Mom and her younger sister, Evelyn, were little. But I only knew a snippet of her story.

Decades later, my husband Roy and I spent an evening with my mother's sister and her husband, Uncle Clarence. After-dinner talk drifted to family history and Evelyn shed more light on the sad faces of the Mamaa and Grandy I knew as a preschooler. Their first child had been a boy. Stricken with pneumonia in 1917, the toddler went to the hospital and died there. In 1918, my mother was born to parents still steeped in grief. A handful of faded sepia photos taken in the twenties show a child with an often-unsmiling face. Grandy was truly a woeful man. A traveling salesman, he was involved in an automobile-train collision that cost his closest friend his life. Then, before the miracle of the Salk vaccine, polio struck my Mamaa.

Perhaps eager to escape a home sagging under the weight of sorrows, Mom married my father, when she was twenty-seven. Evelyn and Clarence had long since fled, marrying in their teens. In his autobiography, Dad wrote that the two of them had premarital talks about shared values including church, children, and family. But did they really speak a common language? Did he just assume she would easily trade off her wartime independence as an Air Fairy support crewmember, volunteer German U-Boat spotter, and fledgling interior decorator — for the domestic arts of diapering babies and baking biscuits?

As a design artist, she dreamed of a lifelong, creative career and married a man who likewise would devote forty years of his life in a corporate climb toward the summit of once-renowned international airline, Pan Am. Did they ever discuss how these two ambitious people would actually raise a family? How long did their romance truly last? My sister and I had no answers to these questions. We saw few signs of playfulness, passion, or joy in their union.

I don't remember when my mother's smiles grew so small, they simply slipped into her scowl lines. Perhaps because I didn't want to remember, early signs of my parents' disintegrating relationship were lost in the persistent storm clouds that built like thunderheads, roiling the atmosphere over our house. It was my destiny to grow up seeking shelter.

Birth of a Monster

The storm originated, like many Atlantic systems, as a lowly wave emerging off the West African coast on August 14. It would become better organized over warm water with little atmospheric influence to disrupt its development.

~ Andrew Krietz, 10 Tampa Bay (News)

Homestead, August 21-22, 1992

The spawn of a stormy marriage of western African coastal currents and wayward winds, Andrew, the first tropical storm of 1992, struggled in the warm waters of the Caribbean. On Friday, August 21, my daughter Krissie's fourteenth birthday, the morning news dismissed the poorly forming storm as "Raggedy Andy," barely strong enough to be considered a threat.

But while we tried to sleep that Friday night through Krissie's slumber party and a typical summer thunderstorm, Andrew was hundreds of miles to the East, grooming himself. While a gaggle of giggling teen girls midnight-snacked on M&M's® and potato chips, he fed on the tropical Atlantic water, flexed his muscles, and sharpened his claws. Then, he shed his baby teeth for longer, sharper fangs. His sudden growth made him hungry and determined. By early Saturday morning, he detected a faint scent from the West, the scent of a mass of human life in the megalopolis of South Dade County and the greater Miami area. Meanwhile, the party girls had crashed from their sugar high and slept peacefully for a few hours.

Aroused by the promise of easy prey, he sucked in great heaving breaths of warm ocean air and began to speed his prowl toward land. A hurricane watch was issued for the Northern Bahamas.

On that Saturday morning, our neighbor, Air Force meteorologist Captain Will Bowman, crossed our street, looking for Roy. He wanted to show him a computer printout of the projected storm path.

We studied his handiwork. In light gray ink on white, an outline of Florida, Cuba, and the Caribbean. To the right of the Bahamas, lay the little curlicue symbol for a hurricane, with a dotted tail showing its earlier track, and a line of dashes to the West, heading "bulls-eye" into the area south of downtown Miami. Will's computer prediction placed us at Ground Zero.

"It's coming right for us," he said. "And it's now a hurricane — winds up to ninety miles an hour."

Roy eyed the map and shook his head. "I think they say it's going to veer north–they usually do."

But my husband was not going to take lightly a threat to the base. He was responsible for Homestead's supply and fuels operations. A storm meant hours of preparation. Will went back to his computer, and we drove across the base to see my husband's troops.

The young fuels specialists, munching breakfast doughnuts, stood around a droning television. Early weather reports now alerted Southern Floridians that Andrew had shown steady and rapid strengthening overnight and was a cause for concern. Roy questioned the timetable for "backfilling" a fuel tank, which was being drained for cleaning. If high winds hit the base, it was critical the fuel tanks be full — and heavy.

"It'll take several hours, Sir," one of the troops replied.

"Well, no official word from the boss yet, but let's go ahead and start the backfill." Roy shrugged, "We can always drain later." He shook his head, "If this thing is less than seventy-two hours out–" He didn't finish.

I felt a chilly nettling around my neck and arms. No need for panic. As a child, I lived through hurricanes. But there were dangers. Tornadoes sometimes popped down from the outer bands, flying tree limbs could smash through a roof or window, power outages could leave us with relentless mosquitoes, survival rations, and no water for up to two weeks.

"I'm going to the commissary to get extra supplies right now," I told Roy, as we left his troops. "Beat the rush, before everybody starts shopping crazy." I already had a standard emergency kit. Still, it wouldn't hurt to buy more batteries, along with extra gallons of water and instant meals.

Homestead's commissary looked like any other grocery store on Saturday morning. I placed my storm essentials on the conveyor, relieved the shelves weren't yet empty. Glancing at the crowded rows of carts around me, I almost gasped aloud. Shoppers were stocking up on gallons of cold milk, fresh meats, eggs, orange juice and ice cream.

"Oh, dear God," I thought. "Don't these people have any idea?!"

Back at home, I called my father in South Miami, twenty-two miles north of the base. My childhood home there was almost forty years old. With its concrete walls and steel-strapped roof, it had proven itself a safe haven before. When Roy's Air Force career brought us to Florida in 1990, we had made an evacuation plan with my parents. We never really believed we would have to put that plan into action. I chattered to Dad about the almost all-night party and our morning activity.

I loved the sound of his Texan drawl, "Hey, along with your supplies, ya'll bring your gas grill in the back of your station wagon." He sounded unfazed. Years before, he'd been Pan Am Airways' hurricane coordinator at Miami International Airport.

"Okay, Dad. See you after church. Let me know if you think of anything else we need." I felt a tiny shiver of anticipation. My children would now know what I had experienced growing up with these big winds: a scary, but survivable thrill, as long as one was prepared.

Still reluctant to really believe Andrew would stay on a westerly course through the next day, Roy and I walked to an evening movie at the base theater. Roy's boss, Colonel Connors, drove up and stopped us, his family in the car.

His face was grim and I overheard some of his remarks to Roy, as I casually chatted with his wife.

"We're standing by for a recall early tomorrow morning," the colonel advised. "Recall" meant all troops would report to duty. The fighter jets would be flown north, to other bases.

"Okay, Sir," said Roy.

"I'm taking the kids to North Carolina tonight," his wife groaned. She rolled her eyes over her shoulder at her young children in the backseat and shook her head. "I'd rather wait until morning, but he says we need to go ahead of the mad rush."

"Probably a good idea, " I agreed, and wished her a safe journey. "See you all in a few days."

We never saw one another again. In the chaos to come,

our lives would be completely uprooted and end up going in different directions.

Roy and I relaxed on our rare "couple date" at the show, then strolled home under a clear, starry canopy. We agreed that it certainly didn't look like a hurricane was on the way.

"Calm before the storm," we said, almost in unison.

Not feeling particularly rushed, we knew that packing overnight bags and securing the household could wait until morning. We watched a late weather report showing a geographically small, but well-organized hurricane formation on radar, still east of the Bahamas. I hoped it would make the anticipated turn toward a more northerly course during the night, and I was not yet afraid for my children, as I whispered "Good night," and kissed each of their drowsy heads. Then, all of us slipped into our beds for the last time at Homestead Air Base.

Feeding on a night-black ocean, closing in from far over the horizon, the monster Andrew pricked up his ears to the rhythms of our peaceful breathing and lifted his muzzle toward the warm west wind. He knew where to find the innocents, and in less than twenty four hours, he would be upon us.

Raging September Sisters

Train up a child in the way he should go; even when he is old, he will not depart from it.

~ Proverbs 22:6

South Miami 1959-1965

"Stay back here."

My father's no-nonsense voice was reserved for warnings or correction of unacceptable behaviors. Dad was a big Germanic man, with a loud booming voice he could use when he needed it. I'm fairly sure his six-foot-two size and authoritarian baritone were partly behind my childhood fear of him. He was not a violent man and was devoid of selfish habits that might have harmed his wife and daughters. My mother, though, held him out like a warning flag when I misbehaved during his frequent business travels. Preferring not to dole out more than a scolding, or an occasional hand-slap, Mom used what is now cliché: "Wait until your father comes home." What an uncomfortable and awkward place for him, coming home to an assignment to punish his naughty little girl.

Like most children, I was curious and possessed by an imagination which led me to telling some preposterous whoppers or snooping behind the lines in my parents' bedroom. Both of these offenses were punishable by spanking, customary in the fifties and early sixties. What is now called "The Greatest Generation," survivors of two world wars and the Great Depression, embraced the

19

Biblical perspective: "Spare the rod and spoil the child." But neither my sister Carol nor I were ever beaten, battered, or bruised. For stealing pink Bazooka bubble gum out of my Dad's dresser drawer, which also led to the discovery and partial opening of a vague foil-wrapped square that I thought might contain candy (all of which I tried to hide by exercising my skills in crafting fiction), I received a switching.

This was the protocol: I was sent outside to pick a hibiscus branch, and my father would switch it across the backs of my legs a couple of times. Whoever said such punishment would hurt him more than it hurt me, is misinformed. I would howl briefly and make a desperate note to my little self: don't do *that* again. I know, by today's standards, such discipline sounds like grounds for calling Child Protective Services, and the practice does not get my endorsement. However, with a brief swat, my father taught me to weigh future bad choices. I craved approval from both my parents, and in those early years, the memory of the sting of a switch saved me from repeated trips down a road to perdition. I did grow up respecting the imperative tone of his voice, and with maturity, lost my fear of him, as he became a staunch ally in storms to come.

Dad's warning to "stay back" commanded me to remain with my mother and sister in the carport in the wake of Hurricane Betsy in September 1965. I had just begun junior high, and we had spent the Category 4 storm in a Miami motel room across the street from the airport. After being left alone in our home for two hurricanes in the recent past, while her husband and protector performed his official duties at the airport, my mother insisted we wait for Dad in a place close by. She lived with traumatic memories of Miami's unnamed killer storm of 1926, which lifted her frame house off its foundation and dropped it a few feet away. In hurricane force winds, tied to one another by a rope, she and her family had battled their way across the street to shelter with neighbors.

Dad's preliminary walk around the yard brought him in full circle to the carport. Our house had no damage, but trees were broken and tattered. He reached inside the carport for a long-handled shovel.

"What's wrong, Dad?" I asked.

"We got a big snake under the living room window."

I loved catching and playing with green "grass" snakes. "Can I see it?"

He spoke over his shoulder as he walked toward the back of the house, "I think it's poisonous. Ya'll stay here."

It was my father's nature to protect us from danger and life's gruesomeness. Aptly named "Arthur," a name that always evoked Camelot and courtly manners, my father was very much a knight, unflinching when faced with a threat to his home. He honored God, loved his country, served in time of war, and guarded his family. Yes, it was an old-fashioned concept: chivalry.

This was a man who cleaned and filleted fresh fish in the backyard and kept me away from the guts. He hunted no other game, so I never observed meat processed from death to dinner table. That day, his sense of chivalry kept me from watching him hack to pieces and bury a coiled diamondback rattlesnake. I imagined the revolting sight and it quelled my curiosity.

"He was probably looking for higher dry ground," Dad explained. "The hurricanes wash 'em out of their holes." Satisfied we were safe, he enlisted Carol and me to assist with yard clean-up, followed by long days of camping out, awaiting power restoration.

Until 1992, my one-word memory association with "hurricane" was "inconvenience." Recalling Hurricanes

Donna, Cleo, and Betsy of the early '60's, I can still smell glowing charcoal on the barbecue grill and mosquito repellent spray, tasting slightly of alcohol, if I accidentally brushed a hand across my lips. We washed our hands and mini-bathed with packaged wet towelettes. The smallest amount of water possible was scooped from a full bathtub for occasional toilet flushing. And without our electric fans, Miami's early fall mugginess hung like a soggy beach towel over us all.

All three events left me with faded mental snapshots of broken landscape and a brief hard life, sustained by bottled water, canned goods, and flashlight batteries. What I call the "September Sisters," all intense storms, wrought millions of dollars of destruction on the Caribbean, Bahamas, and Florida (and later, points north.) [1]Although Miami, Homestead, and the Florida Keys all took beatings in those years, I never heard adults talk about widespread devastation or death. Such details would have been kept from us, anyway. I didn't know then about the hundreds of lives lost. I knew the world from a well-protected child's point of view. Under more than the flat gravel and pitch roof of our one-story concrete block Miami rancher, I was growing up sheltered.

Twenty-seven years after my last encounter with the phenomenon known as an Atlantic hurricane, how could I have suspected the cataclysmic power churning toward us when South Floridians woke Sunday morning, August 23, 1992?

In the Bull's-Eye

Be prepared.

~ Boy/Girl Scout Motto

Sunday, August 23, 1992, 6:30 a.m. EDT

"This thing's coming," Roy announced as I sat up in bed, rubbing my eyes. He was already in his battle-dress uniform. "A category 3 or 4 storm. Winds around 120, intensifying. We're under Hurricane Watch." I wasn't sleepy anymore.

While we'd slept, the monster had never wavered, never changed his course. No longer "raggedy," Andrew, pulsing with enough power to light up a city, was hell-bent for ours.

Without stopping to eat breakfast or change out of my pajamas, I helped Roy lift his late grandmother's cedar chest onto our bed and roll up the Turkish rug off the living room floor, laying it across the dining room table. We woke the children and ordered them to start picking up everything stored under the bed or low to the floor. Roy kissed me good-bye and told me he would join us at the South Miami house.

The television weather droned in the background, as my three children asked endless questions. Board games, books, and shoeboxes were strewn across their beds. I was slipping a plastic bag over photo albums when Krissie poked her head into my room.

23

"What should I do about the air pump for my goldfish, Mom?"

"Unplug it and your lamps too. Leave the top off the aquarium. He'll be okay for a couple of days, I think."

Ten-year-old Jimmy was stashing his favorite GI Joes into his overnight bag. "How long will we be at Granddaddy's, Mom?"

I honestly wasn't sure. Two days, maybe. We probably could get back to our house by Tuesday. "Take two or three changes of cool clothes. It'll be hot if the power is out."

I walked down the hall to check on my fifteen-year-old, Seana, seated in the middle of her teenage clutter: dirty clothes, piles of sketchpads and cartoon art, textbooks, summer reading paperbacks. "Maybe a hurricane would clean this mess up," I carped.

"Maybe." She grinned back, stashing her stuffed animal collection into a large garbage bag.

I ran through a list of instructions and reassurances for my children. I had grown up thinking of Miami's threat of hurricanes as a part of late summer, like breaking in new school shoes and sweating in the September classroom.

"Put towels at your windows and against your doors when you leave the room...rain usually beats in through the windowsills...don't worry, we'll be safe with Granddad and Libby (Mother refused to be called any variation of "Grandmother.") They are in a sturdy concrete house, far from the water...the yards will be trashed, probably lots of tree and shrub damage. We'll be okay." After all, we had always been "okay" in my old home, when the "September Sisters" blew through town.

All three children were unusually efficient, harmonious, and eager to help me. "Mom, let's get the videotapes out of that low cabinet. Where should we put them? Should we fill both the sinks in the bathrooms, along with the tub, Momma?"

I fielded questions, while filming every room of the house with the video camera, in the event of an insurance claim. I kept one ear tuned to the television.

The 8 a.m. update increased the sense of inevitability of the hurricane. Forward speed was almost twenty miles an hour. We could now expect his arrival sooner, the center, or "eye" passing over by dawn Monday. Hurricane warning flags were now flying in the Bahamas.

Roy phoned me at 9 a.m. "You'd better get to the base gas station for a free fill-up. Lines are going to get long."

I balked. "I'm still in pajamas, trying to move the loose tools and bikes out of the carport into the house."

"No, Bronwyn. Do that when you get back! Get the gas NOW!"

"Well, OKAY!" I silently pantomimed a snappy salute to his order. I was beginning to feel out-of-sorts. I threw on shorts and a tee-shirt and ran a brush through my sweaty hair. Light-headed, I gulped a glass of orange juice and grabbed a granola bar as I dashed out the door.

From the carport, I heard the continuous roar of jets, and squinted up into the bright sky behind our house. F-16 fighters thundered north in two-ship formations. Pair after pair, the entire fleet, after-burners blasting fire from their tails, climbed steeply in the morning sun. A migration of giant steel birds, fleeing from the coming storm.

Roy's imperative call did save me valuable time. Although I waited twenty minutes for gas, a line of cars and trucks snaked behind me, far around the block. I listened to my car radio and scanned the sky, a typical August beach-umbrella turquoise, polka-dotted with white puffs of cumulus clouds. Denial washed over me like a cool breeze. Maybe the storm *would* turn north.

At home again, Roy called, confirming that he would join us in South Miami as soon as he could, and reminded us to get off base soon to beat the exodus out of the Keys.

At first, I lingered. Cereal bowls sat in the kitchen sink. Clean laundry waited inside the dryer. But I was not going to take a chance on becoming entangled in the traffic on the Florida Turnpike. We'd just have to leave some chores undone for a couple of days.

My station wagon looked like a village on wheels. Stuffed inside were five cages, homes to two hamsters, a large white rat, and "Pickles" our parakeet, with his new bird-buddy "Foofer," vacationing with us, while a friend of Kris's was out of town. Piled around us were a plastic laundry basket full of important papers, computer software, and a few pieces of jewelry; picnic basket and grocery bags of emergency supplies, the barbecue grill, water jugs — what else could possibly fit? I tied down the suitcases on top of the car, suddenly feeling strong and in command of my young troopers.

One more time, I returned to the house, scanning each room. I wanted to take the pile of photo albums from the dining room table but talked myself into believing they were safe in plastic. Surely, the inside of the house would be intact. In the living room, I bent to unplug a lamp, spied a large book on the floor behind the couch and tossed it on the coffee table. I looked again. A hardback edition of *Gone with the Wind*, a present from my mother. I stared at the title a moment and laughed aloud, "I hope not!"

At the door to the carport, I patted the doorframe, blew a kiss over my shoulder, whispered, "Good luck, house!" Then I closed and locked the door.

"Are we ready yet?" a young voice whined from the backseat of the car.

"Yeah," I said, sliding behind the wheel and starting the

engine. Pulling away from the driveway, I never glanced in the rear-view mirror. It never occurred to me to take a last look at normal: neat rows of military housing, manicured lawns, lush palms and ficus trees shading the yards. . .

Traffic on the Florida Turnpike was dense but moving. We heard radio alerts that all tolls were lifted to ease evacuation. Within a half an hour, we were pulling into the old circular driveway of my childhood home. A crowd of old trees–oaks, palms, and a tall pine–awaited us like family, where they had been all the days of my youth. The water oaks, draped in moss, looked like old uncles, just waiting for the children to run by and pull at their "beards." I couldn't help but wonder if the pine would make it through another hurricane. I had seen it beaten and bending in storm force winds before, marveling that it didn't break. I pictured the yard once again littered with broken branches, and my children giving each other wheelbarrow rides to stay amused in the aftermath, with no television, and darkness coming quickly inside a house with no power.

By 4:00 p.m., Roy arrived and parked his car close to the back of the house. He joined me in helping Dad move potted plants from the screened porch into the living room and spoke so the children couldn't hear. "I just left nineteen guys at the base. They are going to stay in a hardened shelter, inside a hangar. Issued them a jon boat and nineteen life jackets. The storm surge is expected to cover the base!"

My husband and father had argued briefly over the telephone an hour before. Roy urged him to evacuate with my mother, with us following behind him on the highway to Riverview, near Tampa, where my sister and her husband lived.

"Art," Roy had pleaded, "You need to get out of here.

They are expecting a catastrophic storm surge. This whole area may be under water."

"Now, Roy," my Dad had replied as the wise sage, "We are on high ground here in South Miami, far enough from the coast, from high water. We've seen lots of storms here. We'll all be safe."

With only the echoes of Hawaii's tsunami warning sirens in his youthful past, Roy truly didn't know what to expect of an Atlantic coastal hurricane. "Art, we still have time — we can all get out of town." I could hear the adrenaline in his higher-pitched voice.

The difference of opinions pitted the two most important men of my life against one another, and I was torn by my sense of loyalty to both.

After hanging up, Dad had turned to me and placed the decision for our own family squarely on my shoulders. "You all can go if you want, but I'm not going to get out on the highway, with people panicking. You break down or get a flat, they're likely to shoot you for your money and supplies. I can't get your mother packed up and out of here. Roy doesn't know. We're far from storm surge, and the house is sturdy."

I knew he was right. I would have to do my best to reassure my man.

My mother, on the other hand, well-advanced in the entanglements of dementia, watched our movements to secure the loose pots and furnishings from the porch. She sat on her favorite old couch in the television room and occasionally commented on the constant drone of weather reporting and storm preparation tips.

"I wish your father would get a generator," she said for the hundredth time. "And we need a pump head for that well." With every hurricane or tropical storm warning, I had heard this pair of unfulfilled wishes. True, there was a well somewhere in the backyard. With every aftermath, we had managed to exist until Florida Power and Light restored our kilowatts; we drank our bottled water and survived. Clearly, with a bit of a stubborn streak, my dad duly noted her reminders but relied on past experience.

High above the row of avocado trees on the perimeter of our acre, a tall wall of gray clouds was building to the East, the first sign of Andrew churning into the Bahamas. By now, I knew the black and red hurricane warning flags were snapping in harbor breezes along the peninsula, from Key Largo to West Palm Beach.

Barely noticing the supper my father had prepared, we watched continuous radar tracking of the storm and listened to lists of evacuation shelters.

"I'm sorry," Dad told Krissie, "We were going to celebrate your birthday tonight, but I couldn't pick up your cake."

"Oh, that's okay, Granddaddy," she said. "I did plenty of celebrating at my slumber party."

"It was unbelievable up at the grocery store," he continued, "people mobbing the entrance, jamming it up so that nobody could get in. I don't know why they wait 'til the last minute to get their water and batteries. Well, anyway, we'll celebrate next weekend if we have power."

Outside, we heard the neighbors trimming tree limbs away from the roof line. Their buzz saws snarled, as though trying to keep the night at bay. Late summer dusk surrendered to darkness.

We waited. We positioned all our flashlights and candles around the house and waited.

The children began to yawn and fade around 11:00 p.m., and we urged them to go to sleep. "I'll come get you, if you need to be in the hall," I told them. With a vague, "Night-

night," my mother kissed each of them and made her way back to the master bedroom.

As they slipped into their beds, my young ones' sense of trust and calm amazed me. They seemed certain we would be all right. Where now was my confidence?

Too Late to Escape

...to the land of deepest night, of deepest shadow and disorder, where even the light is darkness.

~ Book of Job 10:22

South Miami: Night to Dawn, August 23-24, 1992

In the darkness outside, the leaves had begun to quiver. An intermittent breeze rustled through them. Branches scratched and rubbed against the house. In the eastern sky, distant lightning darted in and out of the towering billows.

We sat in the northeast corner of the house, watching the endless weather advisories, talking, and pausing to listen as the breeze shifted gears, thrumming now to gusts.

P-r-r-raap! The brushing of bushes against the outside walls was punctuated by the tap-tap of roof gravel against the window. So, Andrew had arrived and wanted to come inside. And he was within throwing distance.

Midnight. My stomach ached and I felt like a child afraid of the dark. Around 2 a.m., the lights flickered, the television blipped, and the shrubs swished away from the house, then whumped back hard against the walls. Dust puffed off the row of wooden plantation shutters above Roy, dozing on the couch. From a pair of chairs, Dad and I looked at one another.

"We'd better get him out from under those windows," I said.

The television picture flat-lined.

I felt an involuntary shudder, as my "fear-gauge" inched upward.

"There goes the cable," said Dad. No more visuals of local weatherman Bryan Norcross, warning, instructing, explaining to the public what they were about to experience. Our connection to the outside world was now only the portable radio at my side.

We woke Roy and moved into the living room, a more central area of the house. The girls and my mother slept in rooms protected by wrought iron fortification around the back screened porch. But we'd have to keep an eye on Jimmy's vulnerable corner room, my childhood nest, where I'd slept through the storms of the 'sixties.

Through small glass panels in the front door, I watched rain pelting the walk. With a distant rumble turning at moments to a low roar, gales snapped small pine and oak branches and sent them tumbling down the street. Eerie blue flashes–exploding transformers-silhouetted rooftops and trees. Rounds of gravel came at the windows again and again, rapping like grape shot against the glass.

At 3:44 a.m., the neighbor's yard light across the street winked off. In the kitchen the refrigerator hushed with a bump, as the lamp in the television room blacked out. Now only unearthly flickers from the sky cut through the darkness inside the house. A whining gust jolted the front door against me, and I backed away, my flashlight beam quivering on the floor beside my feet.

My father was pacing the living room like a caged bear. He stopped to look out on his screened porch.

"Better not stay in there near those French doors, Dad," I said, helping him pull his favorite kitchen stool into the hall.

Roy, who will, without a doubt, sleep through the

Apocalypse, had stretched across some porch cushions in the dark hallway. He was exhausted after his tense day of emergency preparation at the base. I checked on my children, peered into my mother's room. All asleep.

Settling on a cushion, I gathered supplies around me: radio, flashlight, extra batteries, and a towrope. No one had asked me about the rope. Perhaps they hadn't noticed. Mother's 1926 hurricane horror was pressed deep into my bones. I was determined that if Andrew ripped off the roof and tore down the walls, the only way he would get to my children would be by untying me from them, as we sought shelter with next-door neighbors.

The wind alternately whined at a high pitch and bellowed like continuous thunder. Radio reports crackled in from daring reporters crouching in cars on downtown streets. From the Hurricane Center at the University of Miami, one mile east of us, came the news that wind instruments had just been blown off the top of their twelve-story building. Last recorded wind gust: 164 miles per hour.

Dad awakened my mother to seat her in the hall. The girls' bed lay close to a large closet, which made me decide to leave them alone unless Andrew broke through a window or door. Once that happened, all seven of us would be piling into that closet. . .

I gently roused Jimmy from the corner bedroom.

He murmured something that sounded like "bad now?" barely opening an eye.

"Yes, honey. Let's go lie down in the hall." He stumbled along next to me, stepped over his dad, and curled up beside me, laying his pillow and head on my lap. I stroked his soft hair and silently tried to pray the Twenty-Third Psalm. I'd memorized it at Jimmy's age. Now I couldn't put the verses in order, the old King James phrases surfacing: "He maketh me lie down in green pastures . . .Thou art with me . . . ."

The wall at my back quaked with a blast from outside. "Yea, though I walk through the valley of the shadow of death. . ." A standing bookcase at my elbow trembled. I curled my head and shoulders over my son. "Dear Lord, please be with us, please stay near us."

I shifted a little. With every window closed, the air in the house was stifling, growing hot. Sweat pooled inside the crook of my elbows, trickled behind my knees. Over the roaring and thumping of unseen debris against the house, I strained to listen to callers on the radio, pleading for advice from the intrepid weatherman, Norcross, as their houses blew apart around them.

"Our roof is coming off!" a woman cried. "Where should we go?"

"Get into a closet or bathroom with a mattress over you right now!" came his hoarse reply.

In dim lantern light, I looked over at my father, seated on his high-backed stool. Tense, he leaned forward, each hand resting on his knees, his head cocked to one side, then to the other, at the sounds around us. Our eyes met and he shook his head. I knew at that instant this was the worst he'd ever endured.

I had trusted his judgment. "Unsafe to evacuate. . .we would be okay sheltering in this place." For the first time, I sensed creeping tentacles of doubt. It was too late to escape now.

"I don't know when we're gonna get a lull," he said. True, we both awaited the quiet space inside Andrew's eyewall. When would we have a few minutes of relief from the roaring blast?

The bones of the old house creaked, and the roof uttered weird metallic groans. We knew now we were being thrashed in the maw of the monster. Down our narrow hall, his searing breath swirled across our legs, then drew back the way it had come. His only access to us was the chimney, but it proved too small for his gargantuan proportions. Roaring in frustration, pounding the walls, his tumult wound down in a final tantrum until after dawn. We would soon learn he devoured others that dark morning, but not Seana, Krissie or Jimmy. It was as though they were tucked, peaceful and trusting, into the arms of Almighty God.

I have long pondered the seeming randomness of loss and suffering in disasters. Why was our family spared the agony of those who lost their lives or those of their children? Isn't "Why, God?" one of the most universal cries in the wake of disaster? Anguished echoes resound throughout our history, begging our Creator for an explanation, reason, or purpose for homes flattened in the horrible hopscotch of a tornado through a neighborhood, for the sudden fatal crash, unstoppable disease, or a random act of savagery or terror. Perhaps we are left to explore the *Why* for the rest of our days on earth. What we know on this earth is limited, but one day it will be made clear. I believe answers will be given when I see my Lord face to face in Eternity, as I now embrace the words of the Apostle Paul: "For now we see in a mirror dimly, but then face to face. Now I know in part, then I shall know fully, even as I have been fully known."[1]

§§§

The "eye" of the storm never did pass over us in South Miami. Instead, the calm center lasted for a few minutes in Homestead. Only when we emerged at 8 a.m. on Monday and surveyed the tatters of my parents' yard, did I begin to focus on how my base home had fared. From what we would soon see there, it was impossible to believe that a few minutes of stillness could have offered anyone even the slightest respite.

But, periodic after-bands were still gusting strong, chasing us back inside. As we reversed course, Dad tripped over a branch on the sidewalk and crashed to the bricks. Roy and I both gasped in horror. As Dad tried to right himself, Roy immediately went down on one knee,

"Wait! Art, can you get up? Easy!"

Have I said he was a big man? To my husband's five foot six, Dad's hefty frame was a challenge. But we pulled him–slowly, slowly- to his feet. No arms or legs appeared hurt.

Dad wore a startled, questioning look as blood began dripping from a gash above his left eye. With a little assist from him, Roy and I steadied him and walked him back into the kitchen to his trusty meal-prep stool.

I was immediately cast into the EMT role, one I do not don easily. Motherhood gave me a crash course in first aid, but my husband often ended up the "first responder" to a child sick in the night or injured at the school playground. He pressed a wet paper towel against the wound, and we looked for the first aid items, fortunately handy in the boxes and bags of supplies for our post-hurricane campout.

We cleaned and dressed the wound as best as we could, applying ice and pressure to slow his bleeding. Once we were sure he was stable, we all agreed that he probably didn't need to be in an emergency room handling life-threatening injuries.

Back in the bedroom, we checked on Mom and sat with Dad to be sure he was not hemorrhaging. More whining bands blew through, and we tried to be patient. Before beginning the long trek back to Homestead, we would have to wait until after the beast had blown himself across the state and into the rejuvenating warm waters of the Gulf of Mexico.

Weather Behind Walls

Whether the weather be cold or whether the weather be hot,

We'll be together, whatever the weather, whether we like it or not.

~ Anonymous

South Miami 1956-1992

While we had weathered the storm in my parents' South Miami house, with my back against the wall across from Carol's old bedroom, I often gazed at the open doorway. Before Jimmy stretched himself across my lap and fell back to sleep, I checked and re-checked on Seana and Krissie periodically, like a nervous mama cat tending her kittens. Until they grew restless with the rising heat in the closed house, they slept side by side in a full bed. At twenty months apart, they were far more companionable than Carol and I were in our youth. Looking into my sister's room always reminded me of our shared journey: at first, mismatched adversaries, later growing into girlfriends allied in battle on the home front, even when "home" moved elsewhere.

That I made it out of early childhood without being "dispatched" by my sister, was God's special blessing. Dad

39

had warned her never to hit me, as she was older, bigger, and could squash me. Sensing this immunity from physical harm, I was a frequent pain in her . . . side. Her door had to be locked when she was not home. She had fascinating treasures, such as a brand-new Swiss watch — a gift from our parents' trip to Europe. Have I mentioned I was a born explorer?

One day, while she was at school and the babysitter/ housekeeper was possibly outside hanging clothes on the line, I tried Carol's door. Voilá! It was unlocked and I got to the watch. I had already staged my dainty Swiss tea set in the bathroom. How my impish three-year-old fingers could pry her watch apart, is still a mystery. Time for a science experiment. Would the itty-bitty parts of her watch float in teacups full of water? I never really had time to summarize my findings.

Caught! Wet-handed! So loud was Carol's howl at the fate of her precious watch, the immediate aftermath is a dim memory. Maybe she sneaked a blow to my head before anybody saw? She recounted the tale many times throughout our lives, reminding me that younger siblings should regard life as a gift.

On her fiftieth birthday, I presented my beloved Carol with a Fossil watch with a transparent face, allowing her to account for all its moving parts. Although the reference to a "fossil" on the occasion of turning fifty gave her pause, overall she was delighted. I again thanked her for giving me a second chance at life.

As I navigated adolescence, it turned out to be Carol, and not Mom, who was my counselor and confidante. We were friends by the time I reached fourteen, and was suffering from menstrual cramps. At last, she knew we could be kindred spirits in pain. She showed promise as a life-long pal when she invited me to spend a weekend at her dorm at the University of South Florida. Even better, knowing my love of drama class, she included a live on-campus play in the itinerary. Our family enjoyed live theatre; in the world of make-believe, we sisters shared common ground. On the brink of high school, an active imagination and passion for acting diverted me from the real-life drama under our roof. I aspired to be an actress. Or so I thought.

By the time I had lived through three hurricanes, I began to waffle on my future as a Broadway performer. Florida's dramatic weather fascinated me, and suddenly I wanted to become a meteorologist. The same scientific curiosity that led me as a toddler to dissect a watch told me I needed more information.

Neither parent greeted my startling re-direction from arts to sciences with, "You!? A meteorologist? HA, HA! Go study your Algebra!" In fact, through his acquaintance with a Pan Am weatherman, my father arranged a visit to the National Hurricane Center at the University of Miami. There, I could talk with the experts and see their work environment.

My first surprise was that there was not a woman in sight. Men, mostly in white shirts and dark ties were scattered across a large room filled with desks and green television-like radar screens. One kind gentleman gave me a tour of the room, pointing out where and how they tracked storms, as they received data from a large antenna dish on the roof of the building (eventually to become a casualty of Andrew). Their position, twelve stories above the campus, gave them a bird's eye view from almost wall-to-wall windows. Perhaps the men working there were amused by this skinny middle schooler in shiny penny loafers, but I enjoyed their tour, listened to their encouragement, and one man's suggestion that I aspire to attend Massachusetts Institute of Technology. Most fascinating that evening was their favorite "toy" in the office: a larger than desk-sized tall console with a mosaic of buttons and dials and screens — the most advanced forecast computer ever. It was, after all, 1967, the same year director Robert Simpson joined the men on the twelfth floor. I do not know if I met him that night, but his fame lives after him as the co-developer of the Saffir-Simpson scale still used today to classify hurricane wind intensity "Category 1 to 5."[1]

I raced to the library the next week and looked up information on M.I.T. Alas! The math requirements were a mountain too far. I loved words but hated word problems. "Meteorologist" fell off my list of career possibilities. I guessed I would have to settle on writing and illustrating science reports about weather.

While I found performing in drama class provided me with positive attention, I wrote plays, poetry, and stories for English class and for fun. Bringing home gold stars on poems, contest-winning essays and creative stories, I lapped up my mother's approval. She pushed me to study journalism, assuring me she knew I would succeed with a career in writing. But I was a growing, rebellious teenager, irritated that she was now using me as a sounding board for constant complaints about my father, who seemed to be a decent and godly man. I wasn't going to accept anything my mother "knew best." I hadn't yet considered that one day, I might have a story to tell.

In travel at least, my parents appeared companionable. Much of Dad's airline work was in Central America, so Carol and I studied our Spanish and often accompanied them to Mexico or Guatemala, visiting other families in the business, sightseeing, and shopping local street markets. Mother even had an interior design client in Nicaragua.

Dad's forty-year career with Pan American took us

around the world to many exotic places. We learned to "dress our best" for airplane rides, to eat dinner without complaint to our host at 10:00 p.m., wake at 1:30 a.m. to catch a flight to Bangkok or Beirut, and drink Cokes all day, if the local water caused "traveler trots." Cancelled flights or unplanned stops due to jet engine trouble didn't rattle us, as we visited company friends scattered around the globe. We still call them today "The Pan Am family."

Our gregarious father loved to entertain, filling our home with visiting travelers and business associates of all colors, creeds, and nationalities. Some of his local Pan Am friends were like aunts and uncles to my sister and me. Our actual extended family was small: Dad's two Texas brothers and their families rarely visited Florida. Mother's sister, Evelyn, husband Clarence, and their three boys, lived many years in Chicago, and later North Miami, which despite the name, is not a short hop to South Miami.

Our Christmas mornings sometimes featured an open house brunch, with "compadres" who had known my parents since the Venezuela days. Popular in the fifties and sixties, too, were cocktail parties, which I found dazzling in colors and culinary delight. A long kitchen counter bar featured mixed drinks, fizzing and swirling with green olives, lemon and lime wedges, maraschino cherries, and pungent little pickled onions. As feeding people was one of Dad's "love languages," he set out buffets of peeled shrimp bowls, roast beef, cheese boards, finger-sized sandwiches with ham, chicken salad, and pimiento cheese. Besides colorful bakery cookies, half-dipped in chocolate, freckled with pastel sugar, there were often surprise desserts such as flambéed Cherries Jubilee –a brief festival of firelit liqueur against the dark red-purple fruits, in a thick syrup poured over vanilla ice cream.

Behind the scenes, though, bubbled a stew of anxiety.

Mother bristled at entertaining. Her chosen career allowed her to work quietly with one or two clients at a time. Usually, the prospect of guests — even her one sister's family – agitated her. She fretted over all the details of hospitality. Somehow, our spacious home and welcome mat were never enough.

"There aren't enough matching dishes — or glasses," she'd say.

Dad would shrug. "So, we can use paper plates."

This would launch her into an angry rebuttal. He was sincere. Casual was as good as formal. She demanded symmetry and style. Battles ensued as my father's long-suffering personality only went so far. Up went his volume. Down the hall went my mother, often dissolving in tears. From my childhood perspective, these were no "discussions;" they were verbal warfare.

Yet when the house was full, their friends' cigarette smoke drifting overhead, ice tinkling in glasses, Mom appeared to forget her own protestations and enjoy their company. Carol and I were confused at having two mothers in one. The sad-eyed woman in slippers and drab housecoat who retreated to the bedroom, would later metamorphosize into another lady, swishing into the living room in a silk dress, bedecked in bright gemstone jewelry, blue eyeshadow and red lipstick, hair and nails professionally done. She would arrive a few minutes late and bask in their friends' attention. The latter eventually disappeared with age and profound depression, as she withdrew more and more, sometimes even refusing to come out to join a family gathering. My father would excuse her with, "Liz isn't feeling well." Most of our family and close friends knew the truth.

Anxiety and agitation had plagued our mother for years. Despite the help of Alberta, a beloved housekeeper photographed holding me as a newborn in her arms, Mom struggled in her maternal role. Women and their physicians didn't even talk about "postpartum depression" in the early fifties. By her own admission, I learned that once I could toddle and find trouble, with boundless energy not given my sister, mother's Dr. Walsh told her she "needed to get back to work" to avoid a nervous breakdown.

It was an era when many women who settled into married life following their "Rosie the Riveter"- style contribution to the war effort found domesticity too stressful. New drugs promised life with ease, and my mother trusted the authority of her good doctor. To help her cope, Mother began taking the popular relaxant, Miltown. Despite her talent for designing color-coordinated, classy, and elegant spaces, including Pan Am's Clipper Club in Miami International Airport, she could not find harmony and balance in her own mind and body. With one prescription after another, she careened down a slow journey into dependency and hunger for stronger relief for the rest of her life.

Whatever she was taking, it must not have been enough. Images of the young woman, evocative of beautiful actress Vivian Leigh of *Gone With the Wind* fame, the smiling coquette who once loved to dance, had disappeared amid my preschool photos. Often, I was puzzled over the genesis of my parents' intense arguments. I never heard accusations of infidelity, gambling, or risky business schemes. There were money rumbles about excessive credit card use. My mother had grown up so poor that she rebounded with lavish spending on tailored clothes, jewelry, shoes, and handbags; she spared no expense providing plenty of clothes for Carol and me. But whatever the topic, every disagreement escalated to loud, angry arguments, sometimes screaming, and I hid behind my closed bedroom door, hearing threats that frightened me.

"I'll *kill* myself," she would cry.

Then his voice, turning low and uncharacteristically soft, "Elizabeth, don't talk like that."

"I *will!*"

Then torrents of tears and an unrelenting pall that shrouded our house for years.

I must have been terrified she would leave. My sister tells me that when I was about seven and she was fourteen, following a bout of verbal fireworks, Mom did leave us for about a week and lived in a YWCA, an inexpensive shelter for women in that era. I have completely blocked that memory. Other events still well up from my deep past, possibly as far back as two-years-old: the taste of sweet, creamy formula from a warm bottle, and the fuzzy snuggle of Pal, the family dog, who died when I was three. But as I grew, I became a regular Houdini at working myself free of the dark boxes and bindings of the raw fear of abandonment.

Avoidance took many shapes throughout my childhood: turning up my radio, reading in the bathroom with the fan on, running outside to perform "skin-the cat" maneuvers on the swing-set trapeze, or fleeing to a neighbor's house to find a playmate. By not talking about the "war on the home front," I publicly pretended it didn't exist. I lost myself in fantasy, acting out *Peter Pan* and *Cinderella* with neighboring children. How I wished I could fly up over the roof from a folding lawn chair or be spirited away by a handsome prince on horseback, riding off to our "happily ever after."

Once, Carol shared a memory with me about arriving home after school, horrified to find the word "PSYCHO" scrawled across the bathroom mirror in red lipstick. She wanted to remove it, but feared reprisal. With such drama playing out in many diverse acts, Dad would try to allay her fears, saying, "Your Mom's having a hard time; she'll get over it." Again, seven years younger than my sister, I was often unaware of the dark intensity of Mother's psychological struggles and possibly shielded from some of the real-life drama.

During these formative years, though, I had a recurrent dream of an ugly little demon who sat in my child-sized rocker in the living room and lured me toward him with a green glow down our hallway. Always, I would see myself rise from the bed, follow the beam of eerie light, and turn the corner into the living room. There, rocking furiously in my little mahogany chair, the grinning fiend leered at me with large reptilian eyes, and I would wake, drenched in sweat, my mouth wide in a silent scream.

For years, I failed to make any connection between my dream and the tense reality when I was awake. I can't help but wonder if the rage and unhappiness tormenting my mother in her waking and dreaming somehow infected the house with a grim spirit. As adults, my sister and I have pondered her past. What must her girlhood have been like with a wheelchair-bound mother needing constant care and her father denied normal physical intimacy with his wife? Was Mom tormented by shadows and memories of abuse? What ghosts haunted our home? No answers came. But parents' ghosts can scare children away.

While Dad listened to our problems and often offered suggestions for solving them, Mom's communication was one-sided, a stream of constant criticism. She disapproved of chorus or drama rehearsals on school nights, and disliked our choices in music, movies, and television. She'd had full control over decisions for us as little girls, but struggled with allowing us space to grow up. Our taste in clothes was too faddish and our skirts too short. Most back-to-school shopping trips ended with shirt-waist dresses that Carol once labeled as "suitable for forty-year-old women." It would take us years to be grateful that she wanted to treat us to new clothes and shoes, something she hardly knew as a child during the Great Depression.

Her own wardrobe was full of custom-made dresses, jackets, and skirts. She had a penchant for gorgeous shades of teal and turquoise, rose and coral. After my birth, she wore no long pants, perhaps because she was a short-legged five-foot-three and sensitive about her full hips and thighs. Her formal dresses were dazzling, and I dreamed of getting to wear some of them, along with her elegant high-heeled shoes.

Once, I attempted to compliment my mother, when she was dressed like a fairy tale princess in a snowy satin strapless gown with a bright fuchsia sash wrapped across the bust and sweeping down the back of the train.

"You look sexy, Mom," I said, waltzing around the living room with my father, my sock feet balanced on the tops of his shiny dress shoes.

She rebuked me: "Well, that's not a nice thing to say. That's not a nice *word*."

I thought I was saying she was stunning. Somewhere in my childhood, I had perceived that bare shoulders were beautiful and alluring. My internal censor began to quieten my voice.

In Sunday School, I sang that Jesus loved me, but the music of my mother's affection for me clanged more and more discordant. Her love was unpredictable and inscrutable. In the early years, I'd clung to her, wherever we went. "I want to sit next to *Mommy*," I would whine. I don't remember when she stopped chuckling as she pulled me alongside her, calling me "Tootie," a term of endearment she no doubt heard throughout the war years. Somehow, we lost our fragile bond, destined never to enjoy true mother-daughter friendship. Instead of conversations, we would fire verbal salvos.

By my junior year of high school, I didn't want to go anywhere with her. I devoted myself to school life, rising to elected offices in National Honor Society and Future Teachers of America, striving for academic excellence, and pouring my creative energy into Thespian Troupe drama productions, balanced by sleepovers with gal-pals, and trips to Crandon Park beach. Then, an abrupt detour: the unrelenting storm of my mother's depression suddenly dropped off my radar.

Just before Easter 1970, Dad announced a career turning point: a choice between a promotion to New York City, supporting Pan Am at Kennedy and LaGuardia airports, or a step up to wrangle violent labor union disputes with management in Honolulu, Hawaii. Tough decision. Two different worlds: the hammering, honking, pressing population of a city that never sleeps versus a Polynesian, lolling volcanic island basking in a turquoise sea.

Perhaps hoping for a more peaceful life, along with healthy career advancement, Dad traded the Atlantic Seaboard for Pacific trade winds. The only home I had ever known, along with some friendships begun in kindergarten, would soon be 4,854 miles in our rear-view mirror. My "sweet sixteen" year turned bitter.

My friends, though sad to say good-bye, tried to cheer me up with optimism: "Ooh, my gosh, you can learn to dance the hula! . . . Hey, you'll probably meet a handsome beach boy. . . You'll get to learn how to surf on real waves!" (South Beach combers were mere ripples, by comparison.)

All of these opportunities sounded good, in theory.

But the thought of leaving the summer before my final year of high school came like a sucker punch, knocking the wind out of me. The news sent seismic waves through my gut, and I felt sick for several weeks. I would most miss my friend Sarah, whom I'd befriended in the eighth grade. We had grown inseparable in high school, empathetic and united in the pain of struggling mothers. Hers was a widow, left alone with three grown sons, Sarah, and her youngest brother.

My friend and I had bonded the summer we were fifteen. Along with my first boy-crush, a senior thespian from another high school, I taught summer drama for children at the local junior high and Sarah played piano accompaniment for our adaptation of *Oliver!* For hours, we were together, creating costumes and choreography. Standing alongside her piano, I rehearsed the songs of the female lead in the show, and together, we giggled and made much of the on-stage love affair between Dickensian villain Bill Sikes and his "good-time girl," Nancy. My co-actor and fellow teacher, I'm sure, didn't give me a second thought outside the theatre. After all, he was a man of seventeen!

The following year, we had a circle of girlfriends, who had sleepovers where no one slept, and beach parties with boys who liked to sing folk songs and play guitars. Behind the music, we learned some of our mutual friends were experimenting with drugs, though not at our gatherings. I was barely aware of this penumbra in our social sphere. Perhaps, I hadn't any spare emotional space for my peers' pain. The announcement of the transfer to Hawaii landed with a thud in Sarah's and my world. We didn't know our friendship was for life. When one is sixteen, it's easy to be tangled in the thicket of "right-now."

The Best family was leaving the threat of Atlantic

hurricanes behind. In the coolness of mountain breezes, I would soon learn that in Hawaiian, *Aloha* means not only "goodbye," but "hello." On a small rock, a part of a long archipelago in the middle of a deep, deep azure ocean, I was destined to discover a third meaning of *Aloha:* "love." But the wild winds within our home did not end with the move. They were, after all, part of our baggage.

Surrounded by Water

No man is an island entire unto itself.

~ John Donne

Hawaii 1971-73

"Hold it!—Smile!" said a photographer positioning his large, professional camera. A non-stop trade wind whipped through my pixie haircut, turning it into a small wild shrub. I grinned, a conditioned reflex.

Snap-Flash! My seventeenth year began when my feet landed on the tarmac at Honolulu International Airport. Posed at the wing's edge of one of the first Boeing 747 jumbo jets in the industry, I stood in evening darkness, bleary-eyed and blinded for a moment by the flash-bulb. My smiling sister and Dad, who had already spent June and July on Oahu, greeted me with kisses and a triple carnation lei around my neck. The breezy air mingled sweet floral fragrance with jet fuel.

"Ah-lohh-Ha!" they said in unison. I was certain my Dad wanted me to feel like a celebrity, fresh from starring in my last summer drama production in Miami. I was touched by his gesture. After all, as *The Beatles* launched their first U.S. tour, they posed under the Pan Am "blue globe" tail logo, soaring high above their iconic bowl-cut hair. Why not me, too?

After the initial onset of "Polynesian paralysis," the

lethargic adjustment all mainland U.S. travelers experience in Hawaii after crossing several time zones, reality settled in. Despite my efforts to be a good daughter, take-it-in-stride, adjust to circumstances, and follow the advice of all the other maxims I'd been taught as an airline brat, I sank immediately in fathoms of sadness. Oahu's lush beauty in rainforests, verdant flying-buttress mountain ridges, and the heady scent of exotic ginger, plumeria and pikake, were no consolation as summer ended. My "besties" mailed their wallet-sized graduation portraits to me. I wept over them.

Wafting through the streets of downtown Honolulu, the rich blending of Asian-Pacific and European cuisines touted grilled teriyaki steak, fried mahi-mahi, garlic shrimp, ginger chicken, coconut, and fresh wedges of home-grown pineapple, but I wasn't hungry. Awaiting the first day of school in a small, silent rental house, I starved for companionship while my father and sister worked across the island at the airport. Carol wrapped up two months of waitressing at an airline terminal coffee shop, before going back to finish her degree in Tampa. We practically passed like the proverbial ships in the night. I missed her.

The Koolau mountains leaned close and friendly, almost into our lanai. Even so, I soon grew bored watching clouds roll up the ridges and over the emerald summits like white dolphins. Frequent rains on the windward side of Oahu opposite sunny Waikiki Beach came as a surprise and often halted my attempts to sunbathe. Passing the hours, I wrote to Miami friends, read the *Honolulu Star Bulletin*, watched TV game shows, and resorted to following *Dark Shadows*, a creepy soap opera featuring vampires. Mynah birds strutted around the yard, often chattering and shattering the silence of my days, which seemed interminable until Dad arrived home from work.

The self-centeredness of adolescence fogged my vision. The transfer piled up huge losses for my mother. Miami had been her lifetime home, interrupted by departures for design school and two brief Pan Am assignments to South America and Houston, Texas. She was alone, closing out her decorating business, which had foundered for several years and making arrangements for the property management of the house. Her mother, my Mamaa, was in her last year of life in a nursing home. From my selfish perspective, I thought Mom was dragging her feet. We couldn't choose our new island home until she arrived. My senior year at Kailua High School had begun and we waited for her. Pining still for my old social circle, I redirected my sorrow over our transfer toward her.

She hadn't been in Hawaii long before I was in trouble. To my surprise, although it appeared she spent all day in bed, while I was at school, she had been in my room. Snooping. She discovered my large wall-sized calendar, where I had been journaling short impressions of each day since our arrival in Hawaii. There it was in five bold block letters: my mother compared to a female dog. Instead of running away, I had rebelled by scribbling harsh words. Dad told me I needed to apologize to her. How I seethed at having no private space to sort through my grief! But I did what I was told, and grew in wisdom. I learned to talk out my angst with newfound friends and self-censored my journal entries. She *had* suggested I become a writer. My vocabulary, however, still needed some refinement.

Our stored furniture eventually came off the boat in Honolulu Harbor and familiar things filled our new home in Kaneohe, not far from my school. Providing the comfort of the familiar were the walnut dining table and chairs with turquoise leather seats, the long rust-colored Victorian sofa with two rolled pillows tucked at either end, and my mahogany secretary desk we would one day salvage from Homestead. Yet, despite her love of our furnishings which she once claimed, "could be trusted because they don't hurt you," my mother was no less depressed than when she left Miami. Tempests under our roof were, if anything, exacerbated by the move. She had no interest in resuming her interior design career, refused to drive in her new surroundings, and began to live as a recluse.

Within only two years, another Pan Am transfer loomed, this time to London, England. I declared my independence from Great Britain and my parents, as Roy was now a principal player in our family drama. At the outset of our sophomore year of college, we had planned that we would marry upon graduation—if we could stand the wait. In a rare alliance, my parents protested: we were too young to know what we wanted. . . I was bypassing grand opportunities to travel and study abroad . . . I hadn't had enough life experience to know my own mind and heart. But Roy and I had fallen deep in *aloha*. No way was I leaving him.

That summer our house shook with the gales of change and I was now old enough to remember the scenes I couldn't avoid.

This I have not been able to block out: the hall bathroom door is locked. Mom and Dad have their own bathroom in the master bedroom suite. But, for whatever reason, Mom has chosen to use mine, and has been inside a long time. My Dad is leaning into the door.

"Liz?. . .Elizabeth?. . .E-Liza-beth!!"

No response.

My mother is only fifty-four years old and taking too many pills. Anesthesia for daily living. Up from the souls of my feet, a stabbing pain as if from a blunted needle works its way to my stomach. What if she. . .? Has she finally acted on the threat that I heard her scream countless times at my father: "Well, if you do — (whatever was tormenting her at the time) — I'll kill myself!" Over the years, I had heard my Dad reassuring me and himself, "Well, the counselor tells me that people who constantly talk about it, usually don't."

Mom isn't usually silent in my bathroom.

Suddenly, Dad has a screwdriver. Can't get the door unlocked. While he struggles with it, I retreat one door away and sit numb at the foot of my bed, pulling at frayed threads of courage from somewhere within. She wouldn't. Maybe she has. What if she has?

I don't pray regularly, but I'm willing to try: *Are you there, Our Father?* Back then, I was years away from knowing He would never abandon me.

"Bronwyn!" my Dad calls from the hall. "I need you to help me." He gets the ladder from the garage and I can't speak as I follow him around the side of the house to the bathroom window. It is high over my head and horizontally narrow, with six or seven jalousies which have to be pried out one by one.

"Hold the ladder," he says. I glance to see if the nextdoor neighbors are in their yard. They don't know my mother's true condition. So rarely has she ventured out of the house, perhaps they have thought her absent or unfriendly. They could not know about our darkness. Thankfully, nowhere in sight.

Meanwhile, Dad climbs the wooden ladder and I hand him pliers. He hands down one panel of glass at a time, and I lay them on the ground, my entire body beginning to tremble. At last, he can turn his large head to the side and look down into the bathroom. For a time, we are suspended in this space on an island people call "Paradise," caught like flies in a spider web of time without measure. He calls out to her again. I am back in my Houdini mode, trying to work myself free of these emotional chains. Inside, I am fighting against swelling dread, but Dad's voice brings me back.

"She's in the tub. She's breathing."

Not dead. Not lying in a deep pool of blood. For a moment I am devoid of feeling. Am I relieved? Would it have been easier for all of us if she were at last out of her torment? Now, what kind of monster am I to wish we didn't have to live through this daily maelstrom? I can't face or answer this crush of questions.

My father comes down the ladder and spots my ascent. I must go through the window because I am a hundred and eighteen pounds; I am athletic and agile. But this is strange movement: turning around near the top of the ladder and putting first one, then the other leg through. As I feel for the ledge of the tub with my foot, I lower myself down and finally look at her. She is in her nightgown, lying in a half full tub of water, appearing asleep.

I jump down to the tile and move to the door, snapping open the latch. Dad has already come down the hall; he pushes past me, bends over her, patting her cheeks and calling to her, "Liz! . . . Liz!" He helps her sit up and grabs a towel from the stainless steel bar on the wall. She is conscious and pushes him away as he murmurs "What have you taken?"

As I back out of the small bathroom, my body pressed against the hallway wall, my gut tightens into a giant tourniquet against a tide of anger. *Why would she do this?*

An ellipsis punctuates the memory. Have I turned away from her, where she is seated on the lid of the toilet seat? Have I staggered backward into the hallway and closed my eyes or temporarily suffered blindness? In the short time Dad has gone to get her something to drink from the kitchen and find her a robe, she has stood up on her own, patted dry, and returned to the small guest room where she often sleeps. Her back to us, she is already in the bed. Drained of energy to speak, my father and I retreat to our own rooms.

Afterward, I only remember how desperate I was to cry, to howl. But nothing. No words came. No sound. Strangling outrage has no voice.

Later, Dad shared the story with Carol and referred to the event as "that stunt she pulled." He was frustrated at his inability to protect me from the drama. Always gallant. So much for chivalry. I didn't know then how to console or pray for either one of them. My own fury was my stumbling block. At nineteen years old, I continued to wrestle with a question that only recently found its voice: Why couldn't I have been born to a woman who could *be* my mother?

The aftershocks of her "stunt" left me more alienated from her than ever. I couldn't understand why she only went to sporadic counseling; I stayed perplexed at my father, a man renowned in his work with a large successful airline. Like a tall Texas sheriff, summoned to ride in as a trouble-shooter, he was hand-picked for the Honolulu assignment because a strong leader needed to settle disputes between labor union rowdies and company management. Yet, he could not summon the strength to have my mother committed for serious psychiatric evaluation of her mental state.

Perhaps it was the stigma. The post-World War II generation was not exempt from post-traumatic stress disorder or marital troubles. But the stalwart brand of those who had led the civilized world to victory over Stalin, Mussolini, and Hitler, was "Act tough, keep your powder dry." Socially, you could tamp down all the sorrow you carried with cigarettes and cocktails. You could swill down as many drinks as it took to kill the pain; someone would get you home. Or you could take prescription drugs, whose long-term side effects were then unknown.

For those Baby Boomers blessed to grow up in a two-parent household, the successful man supporting a family depended on his wife to maintain order and keep the kids clean and respectful, especially at school, where they were considered a reflection of their parents. If he was surging forward in his career, the primary breadwinner was expected to have a supportive wife, and not be bogged down in her emotional ups and downs.

Each summer before I married, from Oahu to Great Britain to Long Island, New York, Dad expected me to come home, as my parents carried their tempest from one island to another. In those brief years, each Pan Am transfer was another promotion for my father and a continued nosedive for my mother.

On a warm July afternoon, less than a year from my wedding day, Dad and I walked and talked on the shady avenues near their Roslyn Heights rental on Long Island. After asking about my summer courses at C.W. Post University, he confessed his feelings about some of the hard stuff he and Mom had been through.

"Your mother was a pretty girl," he began. "We enjoyed being together, but I knew she'd had a rough time growing up." Saddened by her history with Mamaa and Grandy, he felt compelled to help her.

"I wanted to make her happy," he said.

Ah, the "rescuer." Sir Arthur, the knight, to save the fair Elizabeth, damsel in distress. Though young and inexperienced in love, my heart burst. I'd always sensed it, but I had never heard him say it.

His head shaking, he continued to lament, "I've never known anyone to cry like she does."

It was true. She could lie in bed and weep for hours, refusing to be consoled. Once, that summer, I heard her cry out, "Daddy! Daddy!" The mystery surrounding her past life led me to pondering horrors I didn't want to imagine. Between her threats of divorce or suicide, I lived braced for impact, even dreaming one night that I woke to look out from my second story window into the moonlit oak trees to see her hanging dead from one of the branches. Her face was blue, and I startled awake, my pillowcase wet against my cheek.

Was I the only one having nightmares? I couldn't fathom how he could live with her illness, find restful sleep, and survive in his challenging work.

As we walked side-by-side, he at last let the truth spill out onto the pavement beneath us. I was old enough to be a wife myself and to understand a little better how he had struggled. He had failed in his rescue mission. The wreckage still burned after all these years.

Dad had reassured me more than once, "I'll keep trying to get her to see her counselor regularly." His tenacious hold to his marriage vows and keeping our family intact taught me the reality of the commitment he refused to surrender: "For better or worse, until death do us part." But he was a broken man of his word.

Years would pass before I learned about codependency. Mom's weakness made him feel strong and needed. Such a marital relationship as theirs required not one, but two parties contributing to such dysfunction. By the time I reached my forties, I recognized that relinquishing my unintentional role as the mediator between my parents preserved my sanity.

I now believe Mom's traumas that came long before

Taffy Tucker met Art Best, were deep and tangled inside her like a cancer. Only dementia, in its ironic erasure of past memories and events, quelled her turmoil and gave her peace in her last years.

§§§

As the winds of Andrew quietened on the morning of August 24, 1992, twenty years after fearing my mother had killed herself in that bathtub in Hawaii, I longed to be able to sit beside her and feel a calming hand on my back. I wanted to tell her how hard my heart was pounding and how scared I was, wondering what happened to our home. But I had learned long before, I couldn't lean on my Mama. I hadn't leaned on her for most of my life.

My own children hovered nearby, waiting for the first news of Homestead's fate. Taking comfort in their young arms, their sleepy faces pressed to mine, I told them I understood their fears. A flood of relief and thankfulness overwhelmed me; I could be there for my children in a way my mother never could be for me.

Mom would live more than a decade after Andrew and remember none of it. We, on the other hand, would never forget the chilling silence in response to Roy's first attempt to listen for proof of life from Homestead Air Force Base.

Welcome to Hell

When you pass through the waters, I will be with you; and through the rivers, they shall not overwhelm you; when you walk through fire you shall not be burned, and the flame shall not consume you.

~ Isaiah 43:2

August 24, 1992, Mid-Morning

"Falcon One, this is Falcon Six. Come in, please."

Nothing. Not even a static crackle.

I sat beside Roy on my parents' porch, watching his anxious eyes shift about the room, as he listened for the elusive return voice over his walkie-talkie, nicknamed "the Brick."

Outside, the dangerous gusts were over. Again, we had crept out and discovered that other than some broken and uprooted trees, my childhood home and Roy's car had been spared. Now the air filled with chittering of distraught birds trying to relocate nests. Above the drone of a distant generator, the neighbor's electric saws already whined at the mess of Andrew's wake. But from Homestead, silence.

"Falcon One, this is Falcon Six. Do you read, over?" The commander of the flying wing at the base, Colonel Connors, and fifteen other Air Force personnel had spent the night in a supposedly stormproof hangar. No one was responding to Roy's calls.

Our sleepy children gathered around us. Seana turned up her portable radio.

"Listen!" she said.

"It's unbelievable!" a female voice squawked above helicopter clamor. "We're over the base." I felt my breath quicken.

"A lot of roofs are gone — housing looks pretty hard hit. It's just total devastation — unlike anything anybody expected."

She may have said more. I don't remember. Roy sat numb, the Brick still poised near his mouth.

"What if they're all dead?" he whispered.

"Maybe you're just not getting through," I said.

"No," he insisted. "I've gotten through from here before." Mouth pressed to the walkie-talkie as though hoping to breathe life into a responder, he called to the Commander several more times, each time growing more agitated, moving to the edge of his chair. "I want to get down there."

"Not just yet," I said. "The roads are probably blocked with debris and I'm sure they don't want people in the way."

"I've got to get down there. What if they need help?"

I didn't want him to be a hero. I wanted us to stay together with the rest of the family and wait for someone to tell us it was safe to return to a place already described as "devastated." Overnight, just outside the door, the neighborhood had turned into a jungle of downed power lines and massive tree roots clawing at the sky.

"Maybe we can get to our house!" Roy said, jumping from his chair.

Reluctant, but determined that my husband was not venturing out alone, I agreed to go along. With a jug of water, a flashlight, and video camera, we inched our station wagon down the street, which neighbors had already cleared to allow a single lane of traffic, if one didn't mind the branches scraping the car.

We left our children with my parents, despite the youthful chorus of protests: "Oh, can't we go? . . . Please let us go see!" Our instincts to protect them from the initial trip back to the base would prove wise. Though we had traveled this way many times, the miles of the Florida Turnpike between Homestead and South Miami grew bizarre, unfamiliar and threatening. Four lanes southbound had turned treacherous, with sprawling steel spans that only the day before held signs above our heads; smashed streetlights and scattered debris across the lanes made it appear as though truckloads of construction materials had overturned and scattered their contents. Once, distracted by the panorama of entire blocks of crushed houses and pine forests stripped bare, on both sides of the highway, we almost impaled the car on a shaft of metal jutting into our path.

The tires crunched through the remains of the toll gates. They looked like the scene of a shootout: glass scattered, signs crumpled, tatters of toll-collectors' window frames tossing in the breeze.

Farther south, the scene worsened. Anything left standing appeared stripped by giant sanders. Cutler Ridge Mall was drowned in a sea of light poles; cryptic abbreviations remained in letters that once read store names like "J.C. Penney." Fifteen stories high, the Holiday Inn was a bombed husk, completely emptied of doors, windows and furnishings. We'd seen images that looked like this before. A page in our history books. Hiroshima.

Rural Homestead's acres of lush tropical plant nurseries were drowned in brown lakes. Sky and standing water seemed hopeless of a horizon. No signs left standing. No traffic lights. Only mud, water, and houses now reduced to piles of lumber, their siding and roofing trusses scattered like broken bones. With windows blasted out, the few dwellings left standing stared back at us, eyes dilated in death. I began to feel I'd survived a massacre.

Off the turnpike, we trekked with other returning base residents toward the main gate. At a corner made impassable by a tangle of low-hanging power lines, we steered over a curb, driving over sidewalk. A 7-Eleven store looked like nothing more than a giant wad of crumpled aluminum awning, with panels of plywood nailed across the entry, spray-painted: "Condemned." Inching the car across the wrong side of the street, we dodged a minefield of glass and shrapnel.

To the left of the gate, nothing resembled the mobile home park we'd passed daily for two years. Tree limbs, scraps of clothing, fragments of furniture . . . nothing in the park stood higher than six feet. I fought a wave of nausea.

To the right, across the street: a wall-sized sheet of trailer aluminum was twisted around the corner of a Subway Restaurant. In a few remaining trees, more strips of metal hung like demonic crepe paper. This was our "Welcome Home Party." A welcome to Hell.

Military police cars limped past us, returning from the Metro Zoo, where they were to have been protected from the storm surge at the base. They looked as though the cops had played bumper cars, then smashed the windshields and windows when the game turned ugly. We parked and stood mute among the other returning residents, all of us shell-shocked. A wild-eyed trooper in sloppy fatigues wandered over from the trailer park and spoke to me like a friend.

"There's dead people in there," he choked. "And a guy trapped with no legs. I can't do anything to help him."

I saw "the guy" with my mind's eye: wallowing in his

own blood, waiting to die. I looked back at his obliterated neighborhood and felt numb, small, and insignificant. An elderly man clung to my husband's arm, crying like an abandoned child. His wife had suffered a heart attack, his house had been destroyed, and he didn't know how to find his soldier son. Roy walked him to the gate guard for help.

The young guard waved off other cars trying to get through the gate, telling them that without official business, they could not yet enter the base. Air around us hung heavy as the odor of an airport tarmac. Having grown up an airline brat, I knew that smell. Potent, volatile, ten times stronger than the faint waft of petrol one gets on an airport ramp, it was JP-4 jet fuel. The entry guard confirmed to Roy that one of the four large "pillbox" tanks, back-filled two days before, was gushing into an adjoining dike. Gashed by flying debris, it now posed a threat to everyone in the area. As a squadron commander, Roy was responsible for those tanks.

"You'd better tell them to put up a 'No Smoking' sign out here fast!" he said to the guard.

A Chief Master Sergeant I recognized from my husband's squadron joined us, laughing wryly, "Yep, if that thing goes, I don't want to be around."

I didn't want to be around either. North, along the still dark horizon, close to my children and parents, lightning whipped to the ground. After surviving the unending night before, I wanted to remain alive now. And I longed to return to South Miami. Curiosity about our own home–less than a mile from where we stood–wrestled with my instinctive desire to stay close to our loved ones.

Soon the guard waved us on base. We headed for the makeshift command post, scarcely able to breathe, let alone speak. While Roy tried to find a path on the main road, I tried to steady our camera. Snapped concrete telephone poles and a confusion of wires and trees blocked almost every route. There was our chapel, flattened. Nearby, the Officer's Club was gutted, with once elegant sofas and chairs disgorged in the entry. Saint Nazaire Boulevard, our street, was strewn with battered cars, more crazy crisscrossed power lines, and gigantic gnarled claws of roots.

Our house! Bravely, it stood, windows missing, half-covered in splintered branches and clumps of foliage. But the missing roof sections of houses in our neighborhood, the totality of destruction we had already seen in a 360-degree scan of the base told us, Homestead was indeed unlivable. We would have to wait four long days, before we were able to get inside and salvage whatever Andrew hadn't pelted with glass or drowned in floodwaters.

At the command post, Roy's worst fears were assuaged when he found his boss, Colonel Connors, and several commanders alive and surprised to see me.

"You need to take her home." Connors told him. "And say 'good-bye' forever."

I panicked at his words, but then realized emergency operations were underway. He needed my husband's help for as long as it was going to take, and I was a liability until Roy could get me back to the old house. I was more than ready to leave the "war zone."

But before he took me back to my parents' house, Roy wanted to try to stop the unstable fuel spill and save any working vehicles from the same area. We followed his commander, driving willy-nilly over curbs and grass, miraculously without puncturing tires. Once in the fuel yards, Roy's boss ordered me to back the car as far away from the gate as possible. I moved at least a hundred yards back into the street and turned off the engine.

Fear flared up on my already raw nerve endings. My

husband disappeared behind a small building; his boss drove away. I was alone, between the ghostly windowless gymnasium and the gas station, with its toppled roof beside me. In the silence, an eerie vacuum, without the low and distant thunder of highway traffic, I continued to survey the ruin of our community. I felt as though I had stumbled onto the set of a futuristic science-fiction film: Camera One pans the devastated streets in a post-nuclear town. Or had I collided with a surreal Dali canvas? A toppled Pepsi machine in the middle of the road beside me, a three-foot chunk of wooden telephone pole knotted in a black wire cat's cradle, strung from one side of the street to the other. In the distance, suspended high above the ground between the poles, a wheeled garbage container, dangling like a dark green corpse.

I began to shake and couldn't stop. Yet somehow, in that instant, charged like the dusky clouds overhead, I knew God's Spirit was present in my terror. Never had I felt like such an infinitesimal speck in His creation. Yet, He was speaking to me. The sound of His voice was inexpressible, without echoes of human speech. He revealed what I cared about. It was not what was left in the remains of my home. I wanted Roy back. I wanted to rush home to hold close my parents and our three children. I didn't care if I walked the rest of my life in the same pair of sandals. Not one thing on earth meant more than the love and sanctuary of my family. Not one thing. Like the Apostle Paul, struck blind in an encounter with Jesus on the road to Damascus, later regaining new sight as though "scales fell from his eyes," I felt my eyes had been opened.

I heard an R-9 refueling tanker growl. Yards away, Roy was at the wheel, trying to coax it out of the fuel yard. Close to the rear of the truck, a madly swinging telephone pole strained to pull up from the ground. Cables from the pole were twisted on top of the refueler. Tugging the entire mass behind him, Roy accelerated, and the tangled wires snapped off the top of the truck. I began to breathe again, and he began down the road. But as he careened forward, I saw the flat right front tire, wobbling along the edge of a ditch.

Like black ooze, the tire was working its way off the wheel. Wild, frantic, I leapt from the car and waved my arms to make him stop.Without a glance toward me, he was singularly focused on maneuvering the truck. I ran closer, my hands forming a "T" for "time out." I was afraid to go nearer and knew that if he rolled the tanker, it might consume us both in a fireball.

Then he looked up and saw me. I screamed over the engine's roar and pointed out the flat. He turned off the ignition. Dusk and a 7:00 p.m. curfew were casting their shadows. Roy swore in frustration, realizing there was nothing more he could do for the leaking fuel tank or the truck until later. It was time for us to return to South Miami for a last uncertain night together for a while. *"Say good-bye forever,"* the colonel had said.

As we zigzagged down the main road, we saw another survivor. A large black dog wandered on the street. He trotted in one direction, stopped, looked around, and raised his nose into the advancing darkness. Over and over, he repeated the same trotting, stopping, and sniffing. Before we pulled away from the base entry gate, I looked back and saw him raise his head toward the low gray clouds and howl— long, low, and mournful.

My vision blurring, I watched him in the rearview mirror as he wailed into the fleeting wind of August, into the wake of mighty Andrew. Stunned and powerless, he howled for us all.

Second Chances

Therefore, I tell you, do not worry about your life, what you will eat or drink; or about your body, what you will wear. Is life not more than food and the body not more than clothes? Look at the birds of the air; they do not sow or reap or store away in barns, yet your heavenly Father feeds them. Are you not much more valuable than they? Can any one of you by worrying add a single hour to your life?

~ Matthew 6:25 NIV

Miami to Riverview, Tuesday, August 25, 1992

The children had twenty questions about school, and I was wondering if Linda Dickerson was still alive. The Florida Turnpike's northbound lanes were crowded with other refugees, their cars and trucks bristling with bungeed and tarp-wrapped treasures. I struggled to concentrate on my driving and listen at the same time.

"Huh? I'm sorry, honey, what?" I said.

Seana looked at me across our parakeet's cage in the front seat. "I said, do you think we will be able to go back to school?"

Linda cut my hair at the Air Base Beauty Salon, just outside the main gate. She and her husband didn't live on base. Did they try to ride out the storm?

"I doubt it, Seana, this is a major disaster. We don't know

71

if the school is even standing. From what we've seen of South Dade County, I don't know. Yesterday, Dad and I could see from the turnpike to Biscayne Bay for the first time in my life. That's several miles. Trees and hammocks that have been there for probably over a hundred years — gone."

"Mom," Krissie leaned forward from the backseat, her hand soft on my shoulder. "Can we try to call our friends when we get to Aunt Carol's?"

"Of course, hon. We'll try. We're going to make a lot of phone calls."

I'll try to call her. What was her husband's first name? How many Dickersons can there be in Homestead?

Jimmy, a rising fourth grader, wasn't going to let his older sisters dominate the discussion. "I'll bet Holy Rosary School *got* it."

"That would be sad. They were just about finished with the new church building," I said.

I tried to encourage my anxious children, "Just think, you guys can enjoy a few more days of summer in Aunt Carol's and Uncle Ralph's pool, while we figure out what comes next."

"When will Daddy be back?"

"I don't know, Jim. As soon as he can get finished with recovery on the base. It may be awhile."

Why had I thought of Linda before our on-base friends? We followed mandatory evacuation orders. They had lived somewhere in Homestead or Florida City, centered in the target-zone. Many town residents didn't leave.

My little boy reached from behind me and played with my ponytail.

French braids were her specialty. People always complimented my hair when she styled it.

"Look at all the lights!" Seana said.

It was only 3:00 p.m., afternoon sun still lurking in and out of the overcast sky, but a stream of headlights rolled south: another convoy of rescuers, olive camouflaged Humvees and Jeeps, probably National Guard. Highway Patrol cars or fire trucks zoomed past, lights flashing.

Now, a line of Georgia Power and South Carolina Electric and Gas trucks and cherry-picker cranes barreled toward the ruin in my rear-view mirror. Honking my horn, I rolled down my window, waved and pumped a "thumbs up" to the convoy. The children joined in, and some of the drivers waved back. My throat was so tight with tears, I could scarcely speak.

"Just look at them. Look at all that help!"

I, too, would be southbound in a few days. We'd made a family decision the day before. My dad advised, "You ought to go over to Carol's where you'll all be a lot more comfortable. I'm worried your kids'll go nuts without TV and lights after dark. Evenings get pretty boring. A couple of days of this pioneer stuff is okay, but we could be a couple of weeks without power."

So, we accepted my sister and her husband's invitation to recover from the storm in their home near Tampa. But as long as my parents needed fresh batteries, bottled water and groceries, I would manage supply runs from there to South Miami.

Memories stirred. I recalled breathless hot nights and candlelight dinners of canned tuna fish, pork and beans, and crackers. Dessert was canned fruit or store-bought cookies. We drank room temperature water from large glass bottles and waited days for a hot bath or shower. I hated to think of my parents enduring a prolonged power outage, but they had been battle-tested. And despite our most convincing arguments that morning, Roy and I could not coax Dad out of Miami. Not before Andrew, nor after. He wanted to stay to guard the house against looters. Mom's dementia complicated travel.

Neighbors offered to keep an eye on my parents. Across the street, Rich Russell reached out to help, even while dealing with his own post-storm trauma. Several miles south, his daughter's family had spent hours crammed together in a bathroom, screaming and physically sick, as their house roared down around them. Mr. Russell was the kind of neighbor who knew talk was good medicine, as were two glasses of Chivas on Dad's back porch.

A semi tractor-trailer growled its gears, hissed in the lane beside me and I startled.

"What's wrong, Mom?"

"I guess my nerves are pretty shot, Krissie."

My body was tight, muscles wooden. I'd awakened that morning feeling bruised. Soreness had rolled in like a tide. It wasn't the external skin that flinched to the touch. It was something else underneath — the skin of the soul.

That morning's events replayed in my head like a film trailer. Was it the throbbing in my chest that had awakened me first or the thrumming of distant thunder? My eyes opened to pale daylight. Sheer curtains stirred over Roy's bed. Heavy raindrops tapped the open windows of the one-bedroom guest cottage, originally built alongside the main house to accommodate my maternal grandparents. It was now a vacant rental apartment and storage nook, and thankfully, a quiet refuge for the two of us.

Lightning winked on the patio, as wind rattled leaves nearby. More rumbling. My heart pounded harder. *No, not again*, I thought. Then, shaking off clouds of sleep, I remembered. It was over. Hurricane Andrew was not coming back.

I moved from my twin bed, crawled in next to Roy and clung to him.He was awake, but we didn't talk. We had been married for seventeen years. Even still, sometimes we didn't communicate our needs to one another very well. But in that moment, tender silence connected us. I tucked my head under his chin, his arm curled around my shoulder, and we lay listening to the clicking drops on leaves, the patter against the window panes. The heat in the powerless room relented every so often to the breeze.

Like a child afraid to talk about a bad dream for fear of it coming true, I held back words. When I was growing up, our neighbors once told me that their father saw cattle decapitated by a tornado. That image was forever imprinted in my memory. With twisters spawned by this hurricane, what might have been sucked up and dropped through our roof? Trembling, I let go of my words.

"I'm so afraid of what you may find in the house. I wish you didn't have to go back there today."

His arms tightened around me. "I know. I wish I didn't have to, either. I've been lying here thinking, I don't believe what we saw yesterday. The base is finished. History."

Silent again, we listened to now steady rain.

"Wonder how bad it is inside the house," Roy mused.

"Do you suppose it's all floating?"

"I don't know, but I hope I can get in today and find out."

The thundershower over, Roy prepared to leave for the base after a quick breakfast of a deviled ham sandwich. In his green and brown battle dress uniform, combat boots, and helmet, he looked overdressed for the growing steam of the day.

"You look like you're going to war, Daddy," Jimmy said. He hung close to Roy's side.

"Just about, Jimmy-Jim," he replied. "You guys be good

for Momma, okay?" Each of the children bear-hugged their dad. "Help Granddaddy and Libby, too."

"We will," Seana assured him.

"When will you be with us at Aunt Carol's, Dad?" asked Krissie.

"I don't know, but as soon as I can."

It was a sufficient answer as the three children, toughened by temporary living and multiple moves in our military life, hung together as a pack and turned to finding some breakfast.

Outside, Roy held me close. He smelled of menthol shave cream and cinnamon gum. I wanted to tuck his scent in my pocket and breathe it in later when I was missing him.

"You be careful today," Roy said. "You're taking the turnpike?"

"Yeah. You be careful, too."

"We've got so much to clean up, I don't know when I'll see you again. I'll try to call you at Carol's."

We kissed and hugged again. His voice turned hoarse. "Bye, Sweetheart. I love you."

Standing on the cracked asphalt of the circular driveway of my childhood home, embraced by the broken arms of the old oaks, I waved as he eased the car onto the street.

"Love you!" I shouted, then whispered, "God, please watch over him."

A chattering green blur overhead surprised me. Homestead's wild parakeets. They had lived by day at the base and roosted by night at Miami's Parrot Jungle. Now fellow survivors, they had migrated to South Miami. A dozen dipped and soared around me, surveying the new torn face of the landscape.

We had often listened to the parakeets squawking and buzzing on telephone lines behind the base house or camouflaged among the palm fronds. They entertained us all, until the day they played "bombs away" in the big bottlebrush tree overhanging Roy's car. At the sight of his splattered windshield, he sprung up a ladder with serious intent to prune — branches or feathers — whichever he reached first. From the safest heights of the tree, the naughty birds stayed clear of the clippers, chuckling at him the entire time.

Now their noisy air show comforted me. God's chatterboxes were safe; our own little chicks were safe. Second chances.

Aquiver with nervous energy, I had found a broom in the garage and begun sweeping leaves and twigs from the front porch, determined to restore order to something. Dad poked his head out of the front door. Although he had not shown signs of a concussion from his fall the day before, his swollen face told the story. Maroon and purple surrounded one blood-red eye. He looked like a battered contender for a heavyweight title.

"Hey, Bron, let that go." He sounded better than he looked.

"Oh, I'll be done in a minute," I told him. "Let me do something before we leave. Are you ready for that x-ray?"

"Ready when you are. I'm sure glad we've got Doctor's Hospital close by."

I drove the short mile to the University of Miami campus, which featured a large medical facility, as well as the National Hurricane Center. The same weather headquarters I had visited as a girl was missing windows. On the roof, shredded tar paper flapped where the windsocks and anemometers had stood their posts, until Andrew hurled them into the Everglades.

The hospital waiting room was full, and as Dad wasn't

gasping or bleeding, we checked in and settled down for a wait. Expressionless faces around us mostly stared at a television on the wall. We were getting our first look at local news since the storm. Here came the litany of initial statistics:

"Five deaths reported so far with no estimate on injuries...fifty thousand or more homeless...predicted property losses in the billions...probably the costliest hurricane in history."

Only five people dead? I thought. Had they taken the sniffer dogs through the trailer park outside the main base gate? I recalled the cry of the distraught, tattered airman standing beside us the day before: *". . . a guy in there with no legs . . . I can't do anything to help him."*

Bold letters appeared across the bottom of the screen. *Homestead Air Force Base.* Aerial views captured blocks of flattened housing and a multi-ton fighter jet ripped from the bolts of its static display and thrown on its back on the pavement. I realized for the first time, disaster video never tells the world the whole story.

Bandages

The wound is the place where the light enters you.

~ Rumi

Miami to Riverview, August 25, 1992

It seemed like several hours in the Doctors' Hospital Emergency Room waiting area, but it was probably a much shorter delay before Dad was called to an examining room. I babbled to the woman seated beside me, pointing at the television. "That's where I live–the base–where I lived, until yesterday."

Odd how friendly strangers can be to one another in a crisis. Two people who would never dream of chatting across grocery carts in Winn Dixie talk sympathetically at the scene of an auto accident, neighborhood fire, or flood. My seat companion nodded and said things I didn't process, as the caption across my own inner picture became clear: "Homeless." She could have been speaking to me in Romanian. I was reeling inside.

I waited, flipping blindly through torn *People* magazines and outdated issues of *Newsweek*. I watched for Dad. My eyes glanced, darted away, and returned to a young woman with a wide, white bandage wrapped around the middle of her thigh. Near the center of the bandage, a faint red stain spidered its way toward the edges. She slumped in her chair, one arm across her middle, the other propping her head, chin in hand. A tall woman stood next to her, shook her dark, curly head at me and fussed.

"She's lucky to be alive. I tried to get her to leave her house, to come and stay with me. She's crazy. Could've lost her leg."

"What happened?" I asked.

"She was hit with a piece of glass, three inches into her leg. She's lucky it didn't sever an artery."

The victim lolled her head back against the wall, raised her eyebrows at me and slightly turned up the corners of her mouth. Limp tangles of hair hung around her pale face; her rumpled tee-shirt and dirty shorts had probably been worn several days. She said nothing, seeming too weak to speak.

Her friend told a long story about the woman's husband flying a fighter out of town ahead of the storm. She'd begged the pilot's wife to spend the night, but without success. When the shrieking wind began to bow the sliding glass doors in her living room, the wife rushed to save her prized piano. She was wrestling the grand away from the doors when they exploded into the room.

"You *are* lucky," I said.

The red stain on her bandage had darkened and widened. I needed a cold Coke. I wasn't sure whether I wanted it more for my damp forehead or my quaking stomach. I closed my eyes. Voices of weary emergency room staff punctuated the droning newscast.

"Greenbaum can't get in."

"Geez, I've been on since Sunday night."

"Did Maria get back from St. Thomas before the storm?"

"Nobody's heard from her."

Was she even alive? I wondered.

The pilot's wife limped down the hall with her friend. I waited, looked often at the TV and at my watch.

Dad returned with fresh gauze taped above his eye. The x-ray showed a small hairline fracture; the eye tissue would heal on its own. His prescriptions included an antibiotic, aspirin, and rest.

"We'll follow up on that eye again in two weeks. No yard clean-up therapy," the attending doctor said, with a slight smile.

At the house, the children complained that they had played cards to exhaustion and were hungry. "Can't we leave, Mom ...what's for lunch? Are you all right, Granddaddy?"

"Granddad has a small fracture, but he's going to be okay. We'll get to lunch in a few minutes and take off for Aunt Carol's," I said, following Dad down the hall to say good-bye to Mom.

She was in the bed, awake and squinting at my father. Her room was dark for early afternoon. "What happened to you?"

"You forgot," he said. "I fell yesterday. Don't you see my black eye?"

She could recite details of the 1926 hurricane: she was eight years old... evacuating a shuddering house . . . stinging needle rain pelting her face. But she could not remember Andrew or Dad's accident the day before. He stretched out on the bed and let his arm fall back across the top of his pillow. I could see he was exhausted. "Isn't it terrible about Bronwyn's house?"

"What about her house?"

"Don't you remember? Bron and Roy went back to the base yesterday and told us they got hit bad by the storm.

Just south of here, the damage is terrible, maybe the worst we've seen."

She frowned. "I think the one in 1926 was the worst." Then, the instant replay of the childhood memories.

She would never forget her story. She would never remember ours. With a sigh, I kissed her goodbye. "I'm taking the kids to Carol's for a few days, Mom. We'll be back soon."

"I hope so."

I left the two of them in the bedroom and walked back up the dark hall, toward the daylit kitchen. I felt vaguely guilty about my eagerness to escape.

The children helped pile up the car with our trappings, including suitcases, pet hamsters, parakeets, and the important documents. Dad came outside to see us off.

"Hang in there, honey," Dad said, pecking my cheek and patting my arm. "We'll be all right. You see how Mom is. It's easier to stay here. We're in good shape for a few days."

Good shape. This from a man who wore a head bandage like a war-weary soldier. He'd always defied discouragement.

"Bye, Granddaddy," the children called out of the car windows. I couldn't speak. He waved from the porch near the door. His smile, underscoring the black eye, looked a little sad.

Toll collectors waved us onto the turnpike, refusing our quarters. We stopped at a rest station, just south of Palm Beach, grateful for working plumbing and a thorough hand washing. In the ladies' room, there was more talk among strangers, peppered with tense questions: "What if we can't reach them by phone . . . How do we find them with the street signs blown away? . . . Did you hear about the Air Force base?"

After our rest stop, I finally told the children that among others, Linda the beautician haunted my thoughts. I then talked myself voiceless for over the next two hours, comparing each of my past hurricane experiences to the horrors their Dad and I had seen the day before. We speculated about where we might live temporarily and what we would do about school. With my bravest face, I told them we would try to ascertain that all their friends and families were safe. I promised a shopping trip to restore a basic wardrobe. At last, we pulled the station wagon into Carol and Ralph's driveway.

They had just arrived from teaching school. A note was still attached to the front door: "Welcome Homestead refugees!" My sister greeted us with her customary "He-ey!" and threw her arms around us. Her tall, quiet husband, Ralph, came right behind her, stooping to embrace the children. Then, he hugged and kissed me, his thin grey mustache brushing just above my lip.

"Roy called," Carol said. "And it's not all bad news."

"Do we have anything left?" Seana asked.

"He made it into the house, and he says it's a mess, but it's not all lost. He says he'll try to call again tonight."

Ralph ruffled Jimmy's hair. "He said to tell you that Andrew got his licks in, but didn't chew it all up."

The call came as promised. "Get a U-Haul lined up, tomorrow," Roy said. "They're going to let people back on base to salvage on Friday, I think."

Friday. A three-day wait to see what was left. . .

"Should I get a truck?" I asked.

Silence.

Then, he told me there wasn't much to pack up. A small trailer was all we would need. We'd lived in a four-bedroom home. My tired throat was strung so tight, I didn't feel like talking anymore. But I had to know more.

"What does it look like?" I asked.

"Well, there's glass everywhere and all kinds of trash and insulation. Somebody else's plastic chair is in our den. You'll just have to see it. Our furniture is all ruined, I think."

"But no drowned critters — or — ?"

He interrupted gently, "Not that I saw. Just mosquitoes. Bring plenty of *Off*."

I scribbled notes to help me focus as he talked. We needed construction helmets, wading boots, gloves, boxes, newspaper, and snacks. Thankful we'd be back together soon, I told him I loved him and that we would pray for him and the rest of the recovery team.

Each of the children took their turn on the phone, reassured that their Daddy was surviving in the "war zone." Tired after the long day, they bathed and settled into their guestroom beds, murmuring hopefully about getting to swim the next day.

Fatigue dropped on me like heavy canvas. I showered, treasuring the tenderness of warm streams of water massaging my skin. For a long time afterward, I lay awake, aching eyes staring into the semi-dark outside the window. The slumbering neighborhood was silent except for cicadas' songs, streets empty and clean-swept, but for the little pools of light between wide shadows.

Drowsy, at last, I craved sleep. Images flashed through my longing for rest. Too many souls were down south, crawling over splintered two-by-fours, and chunks of their walls, salvaging thawing meat from warm freezers and hunting lighter fluid for their grills. So many people in pain. I hurt, thinking of Dad's swollen face, and ached for Mr. Russell's daughter and her shell-shocked children.

I shuddered for the pilot's wife with her scarlet-soaked bandage. . . Too late, I wanted to tell her that pianos don't bleed.

Thoughts became silent prayers. *Father, do you hear me? I hope Linda is okay. Help her, Lord. Help them all. Protect Roy and my parents. Thank you for Carol and Ralph. Thank you for our lives.*

I wrapped the clean crisp sheet around my shoulders, because the air conditioning was cold and wonderful. The pillow cradled my head.

Thank you for this bed and this pillow.

Drifting, my head barely above dream-sleep, I wondered why I'd never before thanked God for a dry pillow, after so many thousands of nights of falling thoughtlessly asleep.

Bring Boots and a Helmet

Happiness is not found in the things you possess, but in what you have the courage to release.

~ Nathaniel Hawthorne

Riverview, Wednesday, August 26, 1992

The next day I raced out early and got the last five by eight U-Haul trailer on the lot along Highway 60, in Brandon. The store owner said he'd not been able to keep any equipment on the premises.

"You can have it for three days," he said, "'cause I got a wait list."

I watched him hook the trailer to our station wagon, connect the wires to the taillights, and offer me several moving blankets. My voice caught as I thanked him and told him I wasn't sure just what we were going to dig out of our home.

"Well, good luck," he said. "Take it easy. Trailer'll bounce a bit 'till you fill it up."

My life as an Air Force wife had been full of abundant surprises and challenges with each move we made, but hauling a trailer was usually on my husband's unwritten list of responsibilities. Where was that confident wife who had so boldly loaded up the day before the storm? I imagine shock has a way of peeling away bravado. When the sky is falling in on us, are we ever who we think we will be? All the strength I needed was trickling into me like an i.v. drip. Surely God was keeping me from collapsing under such unfamiliar weight. I had to believe He would get all of us through the aftermath of the storm. I told myself, "You can do this!" I just had to get accustomed to the jounce and jerk of a trailer on my "six," as pilots call it.

Back at my sister's place, I found the family fixated on the televised news. Andrew had been an unusually narrow Category 5 hurricane. From the Bahamas, it maintained a straight buzz saw cut across the Florida peninsula. The northern bands had ripped through South Dade County, barely missing downtown Miami, but not sparing the towns of Homestead and Florida City, which, from the aerial views, looked like they were a few buildings short of being swept off the map. The storm continued across the Everglades and made a hard-right turn in the Gulf of Mexico, slamming Louisiana with tornadoes before it took its last gasps. Amazingly, the death toll was far fewer that first week than expected. The children and I watched as much reporting as we could stand, mainly trying to catch glimpses of familiar places or neighborhoods.

Slowly, the news bulletins made it clear. We were not going "home" to Homestead. We were now officially homeless, with a forwarding address to a relative's mailbox. I told my sister we could look for a temporary apartment, but she wouldn't hear of it. Ralph already had his mother living with them, but they moved some furnishings around, made sleeping spaces for us all, and never complained about so many Jardins and their menagerie. I'm not sure I had ever been so grateful for Carol and Ralph's generous hearts.

I prepared for the trip back to the war zone, with a stop at the local Wal-Mart. Mom and Dad would need more canned goods and batteries. Roy and I needed bottled water, snacks, and work gloves. First time ever on a shopping list: knee-high rubber boots and construction helmets.

In the check-out line, I jabbered at the cashier like a jittery parrot about the destructive power of the storm, losing home, and returning to "Lord-knows-what" at the base. As I loaded up my cart with my blue plastic bags full, she smiled and said, "Have a nice day!" Two hundred and eighty-three miles from our devastation, it was just another sunny August day in her "Wally-World." I almost burst into tears.

Meanwhile, the children had made lists of the belongings they wanted me to find for them, if possible. My littlest missed his collection of toy cars and the brigade of G.I. Joe figures he'd left to hunker down through the storm. On Krissie's turquoise notepaper was a combination list and greeting card to her dad, a testament to children's resilience: "Love you," she wrote, with a drawing of a cow, captioned: "MOOving time." She wanted her journals, ballet slippers, and an old stuffed dog, "LeMutt," who'd faithfully seen her through ear surgeries and sickness. Seana had left behind brand new contact lenses she was still learning to insert, and hoped for some of her art supplies, a United States wooden puzzle, and books.

Ah, the brevity of their lists! With all my so-called adult wisdom, could I have sent Roy back into our home with a wish for two or three treasures? Perhaps, "worldliness" makes us want more of the world, losing the simplicity of childlike satisfaction. I remembered Jesus's guidance on our possessions recorded in the Gospels Matthew and Luke:

"Do not lay up for yourselves treasures on earth, where moth and rust destroy and where thieves break in and steal, but lay up for yourselves treasures in heaven, where neither moth nor rust destroys and where thieves do not break in and steal. For where your treasure is, there your heart will be also." [1]

What little my precious ones owned was packed in each of their own small suitcases. Two or three changes of clothes, a favorite game, toy or book. They still had two hamsters and Pickles the parakeet for entertainment. Seana's large white rat, "Cleo," had arrived wheezing at my sister's place and succumbed within a few days. Another loss. Perhaps in my own shock, I didn't notice Seana's grief for her pet. She was my stoic oldest child and the quietest. I knew her well enough though to know after fifteen and a half years, she felt deeply, but guarded her emotions.

The new upheaval in the children's lives was turning into their reluctant acceptance of more temporary living. They were seasoned Air Force brats and had done this before—though under far less dire straits. Carol and Ralph's Pekingese "Tai Pan" unwittingly became a therapy pet and lapped up the kids' lavish attention. While they played all day long in their aunt and uncle's irresistible sky-blue swimming pool, with intervals of dog-love, this visit was not ending with a drive back home. Their education for the '92-'93 school year had kicked off with an in-your-face course on "current events." No Sunday School lesson, parental lecture, or grandparent's guidance would ever have so strong an impact as watching their Dad's video, shot on the base on the afternoon Andrew left town.

With newfound wisdom, my troopers had taken stock of all they had seen in a day and a half and made careful decisions about their belongings. I couldn't promise them anything. My pragmatic Seana summed it up: "Just bring whatever you can get that isn't ruined, Mom."

Thunder in the Tropics

He who is not every day conquering some fear has not learned the secret to life.

~ Ralph Waldo Emerson

Miami-Bound, Friday, August 28, 1992

Clutched in my hand were the lists, each penned by my brave "military dependents," who already knew about living with minimal belongings. Before South Florida, we'd had two years in Turkey. The entire family was permitted to ship only 2,000 pounds (approximately a one-bedroom apartment load) to our furnished four-bedroom apartment in Ankara in 1988. Everything else had to be left behind.

"It's all going into storage," we'd reassured our anxious children, and it did.

In 1990, close to 16,000 pounds of stored household goods landed safely at our house at Homestead Air Force Base. How many pounds were left now?

I hugged and kissed the children, certain and grateful their aunt and uncle would love them well and braced myself for the inaugural trip of "Momma versus the U-Haul." My travel companion for my first trip back south was our visiting parakeet, Foofer. Riding "shotgun," he chirped awhile about reuniting with his family the following day. I expected the bird to keep his beak shut, though, about my driving.

As promised, the trailer bounced around a bit, but I minded my speed, maintained control, and made my way to the Florida Turnpike. My "wingman," Foofer, fluffed and chirruped a bit, then pulled up a scaly pink leg for some shut-eye.

I spent much of my four-hour drive thinking about the natural drama of living in South Florida. Miami's "yin and yang" were abundant doses of sunshine and black anvil-topped rain clouds. Towering cumulonimbus billows tens of thousands of feet above, flexed their bulging muscles all day long, until the heat burst into the freezing air overhead and they fought among themselves. These atmospheric bouts were epic. As a child, I was terrified of these storms.

As dark skies rumbled, my earliest memory of scrambling for safety was with Pal, our German Shepherd. He was an old fellow when I was born, adopted me into the pack immediately, and made it his mission to protect the smallest "pup" in the house. My father wrote that I used patient Pal to assist my balance in learning to walk. We were tight.

In a sense he was the first child of my newlywed parents in 1945. The young dog needed an adoptive family in Venezuela when his owner was transferred out of the country. Especially endearing as the runt of the litter, he and my mother became fast friends. No doubt, during her miserable pregnancies, Pal was right there at her side. Years after he died, she often said she wanted another Shepherd, but a small one, like her old buddy.

Black and white photos and old home movies show Pal as no-nonsense sentry by my playpen. I have a vague memory of him diving into leftovers in my cereal bowl, placed on the floor for him — especially with that prize slice of banana I'd missed. Once old enough to play on the floor of my bedroom, I recall the warm heft of his body next to mine as we hid under my bed during afternoon storms. He'd quiver against me, and I'd cling tight, his wiry fur against my cheek. I'm certain we both sensed this connection was our key to survival.

I have no memory, though, of the day that he left for the vet and never returned. Carol tells me our mother grieved deeply for him. I only remember that without my big, furry buddy, I panicked at any loud noise: thunder, fireworks, and low-flying DC-3 prop planes spraying DDT over Miami's monstrous mosquitos.

Late night electrical storms sent me flying from my bed to the master bedroom, just to the right and about seven leaps to take-off and landing next to my mother in bed. Sometimes, for extra assurance, I would crawl between both my parents, calm down and drift off, inhaling the different smell of their sheets from mine. In the morning, I would find myself back in my own bed, arm wrapped around my stuffed red beagle I'd named "Hot Dog." I guessed my dad carried me, fast asleep, in his strong arms and tucked me back in.

One morning, when I was four or five, I stood screaming outside the bathroom door, as Mother got ready for work. I'd detected the distant drone of the mosquito bomber. Soon, down it would roar, just above the treetops, dumping its fog over our house. I once heard a rumor that those retired war pilots buzzed neighborhoods below regulation altitude, and although it might have been a thrill for them, it sent me into hysterics. My mother never did open the door, her muffled voice answering my pleas: "Don't be silly! I'll be out in a minute. There's nothing to be afraid of!" I collapsed against the door, a crying mess. I just wanted her to be where I could touch her.

Firecrackers and Roman candles had a similar effect. When Miami's annual Orange Bowl festivities climaxed after the holiday season, a gigantic fireworks show brought crowds to the old downtown stadium. I loved the dazzle of colors but hated the noise. With my father's arm wrapped around my shaking shoulders, I burrowed into his side, jammed my fingers into my ears and jumped with the explosions. In the usually chilly January air, I needed a warm, close snuggle with the giant man I sometimes feared. In those moments, with all heaven bursting overhead in technicolor, I felt safe in his embrace.

Once, in my early teens, long after I had learned to sit still with my hands at my sides during thunder showers, instead of fingers pressed into my ears (embarrassing for a high schooler), I felt my hair lift at the roots toward a black sky overhead. I was walking the half-mile from Miller Road to our house after riding a noisy, air-conditioned bus from our local mall. Outside the bus windows, distant bolts of lightning darted from cloud to ground. I'd said goodbye to my gal-pal at her stop and almost never saw her again. Alone, I strode for home, with a suspicious silence prickling in the air. Not a mockingbird or cardinal song on the street.

Then, lightning flashed so brilliantly around me, I almost dropped to the asphalt. Simultaneously deafening thunder exploded. I was thin and athletic at that age, but never interested in running. I am certain I set a new Southwest High School hundred-yard dash record without Coach Kynn there to record it. I'm certain her grade book would have gone up in smoke.

Shaking so hard I could hardly put the key in the front door lock, I scampered inside to my room. My old refuge, but without any other comforting presence in the house. Alone, I didn't know what to do with myself, heart

thumping in my ears, fear tangling up my arms and legs —
and I collapsed, spent, to the floor. I knew I was as safe as
possible in the house, but still didn't know how to outgrow
the terror.

Ever a student, I have at last learned that such a profound
fear of even the threat of loud noise is labeled
"phonophobia." Now that I know that it is considered an
anxiety disorder such as arachnophobia or claustrophobia,
light has dawned on moments of my adult life when I have
felt ashamed, as the only one running for cover from the
oncoming oceanside thunderstorm or flinching at the boom
of a ballgame victory cannon.

§§§

Eager to get home to my parents, I was grateful that
post-hurricane traffic into the Metro-Dade County area was
light. Utility trucks and other supply-laden vehicles still
lumbered toward Homestead. I was anxious to steer my
bouncy trailer off the highway. Turning off the turnpike and
making my way to my old home, I wondered about my
mother's oblivion to the current calamity. Perhaps it was
merciful that she was living only in the moment.

The Scroggins family next-door had already picked up
my parents' yard debris. For many years they had done
regular lawn service for Dad. By 1996, they loved the
old place so much, the family bought it when my parents
had to move to Tampa, under Carol's watchful eye. This
was especially soothing to my father, who had seen the
house grow from stakes on a sandy lot in the early fifties
to a well-loved and somewhat worn refuge. Sometimes I
think the neighbors were the angels sent to watch over my
parents in those later years. Unexpected blessings.

South Miami still had no electricity. Without cellphones,

Dad must have been hanging out by the kitchen window for a while, watching for me. He emerged from the front door, jubilant, arms wide for a hug. His brow-line injury was healing, and he especially brightened when he saw the bags full of extra supplies. He explained how Mr. Russell, across the street, had run a string of hoses to provide city water for them. At least they could bathe and have fresh water. What a relief to find mother sitting up on the screened patio, smiling at me.

"Where are the children?" she asked.

"Still at Carol's" I told her, briefly explaining Roy and I planned to salvage what we could from our base house. "It's too dangerous for them to be there. We're going into the house with construction helmets and boots!"

Her trademark squint and a shake of her head as though to say, "Imagine that...?" told me she didn't grasp the impact of my words. She looked pleased to see I had a parakeet in tow, but we would need to spirit Foofer away to a closed room where their cats couldn't find him for a fun interactive snack. Happily, his surviving family drove by to pick him up the following day.

Promising to continue chatting after dark, I stayed a few minutes, but was eager to meet Roy. I kissed them goodbye and left with Dad's blessing and his typical fatherly admonishment: "Ya'll be careful."

Travel to the base this time was considerably easier than the afternoon of the hurricane. Most of the debris had been cleared from the main roads, but I was still stunned by the ravaged brown landscape, mere miles from the old neighborhood. How on earth were people finding one another, navigating streets and subdivisions without street numbers and familiar landmarks?

With my military ID card in hand and U-Haul behind

me, I waited while the gate guard called Roy on the walkie-talkie. Roy's instructions from our last phone call the night before were to look for a blue military truck with the 31st Supply Squadron flag or "guide-on," used in military parades and formations.

Hallelujah! Speeding down the main road to the gate, there he came. Relief washed over me like cool water at the sight of the pick-up truck with the royal blue and yellow guide-on, sailing out behind him. He waved to me to follow as he made a U-turn, zooming back to the house. My heart was breaking the speed limit, too.

Following Him, Finding Us

Actually, the best gift you could have given her was a lifetime of adventures.

~ Lewis Carroll

Rearview Reflections

As of that August of '92, I had been following Roy Jardin from one Air Force base to another for sixteen years. Before that, we spent three of our college years dating one another, sharing two immediate life goals: get our degrees and get married. The fragrance of our graduation leis still lingered when, six days after commencement exercises and military commissioning, we exchanged vows in the Chaminade College chapel, perched on a promontory overlooking Honolulu.

Many of the old Pan Am family flew in, delighted to combine a wedding with vacation in Hawaii. My betrothed's plentiful Portuguese Catholic relatives crowded the pews behind Roy's parents. On the terrace of a military club nestled on the slopes of Diamond Head, Oahu's postcard landmark, we celebrated. At the foot of the mountain, sunset over Waikiki Beach backlit our gathering. All went perfectly until I threw my bouquet over my shoulder and it landed square in the lap of our hired drummer. Running that play again, I sized up the crowd of eager bachelorettes behind me and made a more targeted toss to my right. My right-hand gal, sister Carol, caught it, and the next year, married her Hawaiian wedding escort and fellow Tampa teacher, Ralph Lopez.

Roy, along with an older brother, Craig, had been born and raised on Oahu. He had an extended family that stretched east to the Big Island of Hawaii and California. His father, James, was the baby of seventeen children sired by Frank and Maria Jardin, and his Mom, affectionately called "Benjie," by her sons, was the youngest of six parented by Ben and Mary Denis. Both sets of grandparents had emigrated from the Canary Islands off of Portugal and had come to Hawaii to work from indentured servitude to independence. With so many aunts, uncles, and cousins, a Jardin/Denis soiree required lots of outdoor space and could be heard a mile away. All the family was musical—from washtub bass to guitars, ukuleles, and Roy's drums. They loved to sing and laugh, sometimes perform an impromptu hula dance, and I was soon pulled in by the magnetism of such unabashed joy and camaraderie.

As drum major in the Kailua High School band and a student government leader, Roy enjoyed a wide circle of friends, male and female. Already a glider pilot, he told everyone he would one day fly for the Air Force. Beyond that, he had no aspirations, except to leave his little island and see the world.

When I arrived at the school, I'd seen lots of the world, but felt mine had collapsed. How did one start over with one year to graduation? I eased into new relationships, as I still mourned the loss of my closest friend, Sarah. That was the hardest part of leaving Miami. The world was so big and oceans so vast, never did we dream we would enjoy one of life's sweetest gifts: lifelong friendship, with plenty of time and opportunity for visits.

Hungry to fit in at Kailua High, I gravitated to the familiar comfort of drama class. By December, I performed in an old-fashioned melodrama full of stock characters: the damsel in distress, the mustache-twirling villain, and the "do-right" hero arriving to save the day. I played the hero's mother, silly-in-love with the villain scheming to marry me and get my fortune. It was over-the-top, with excessive goofy giggling on my part. In the audience, the scrappy local boy of Portuguese descent saw me onstage. Evidently, he thought I was cute enough to ask a mutual friend for introductions.

My newfound friend, Jenny, also a Pan Am kid, introduced us in the school cafeteria.

"I saw you in the play," he said.

I set my tray down and slid onto the bench seat across from the two of them. "Really?" I smiled. noting his dark curls and squinty, mischievous eyes. Clark Gable eyes. "How did you like it?"

"It was okay," he said.

Whooosh! Thunk!

My cheery cgo-balloon deflated and fell at my feet.

My internal monologue ensued: *Nice, real nice . . . Rob, was it? . . . Rory? . . . Whatever your name is, you just don't get it, do you? "Okay"' is a "Bombed-on-Opening Night" review. And, by the way,* Rosco, *I'm an unhappy senior whose dad just moved her across a continent and dropped her in the middle of the Pacific Ocean. I'm traumatized. You are not helping. Cute,* Mr. You, *but clueless!*

Do you say thanks to the compliment: "It was okay?" After decades, I still have no answer.

Memory fades a bit. I'm sure I smiled politely, scanned my lunch, and ate my cookie first.

He kept grinning at me, and I made small talk, mostly to

Jenny, while sucking down school spaghetti and cold green beans.

"I gotta go," I said, getting up, tray in hand. "Nice to meet you," I lied to Roy, again with a crocodile smile, supposing that was the end of it.

Without creepiness, he "stalked" me for several weeks: we'd cross paths in the library or join common friends during break time under a large spreading Koa tree. Sometimes we raced down twin steps of a split portable classroom when our respective English classes ended. Our greetings consisted mostly of "Hi!" or in the local island style, "Howzit?"

Once at the foot of the portable, when he asked me to go to a movie, I thought he meant a group-thing, with the "under-the–Koa tree" crowd. That is, until he said, "What time should I pick you up for dinner?" Awkward pause. Then, I accepted a first date with this handsome, fresh kid who would not be nominated for "Most Likely to Succeed in First Impressions."

Many years later he told me he enjoyed my performance in the melodrama but didn't want to give me a "big head." I'd forgiven him anyway, by the first date, seeing the pink tea rose he placed on the passenger seat of his Volkswagen bug. Once, he also confessed he fell for me partly because of my "cute Southern accent." I argued Miamians don't have Southern accents. He probably heard the "Ya'll" I learned from the Texas side of the family. According to him, it was magnetic.

Sharing a common love of movies, playing tennis, and body surfing, we began to date. He took me to an evening ecumenical Bible Study with other students and encouraged me to attend the nearby Methodist Church, even if my parents didn't. Several times he took me there on Sunday morning, as he had attended his Saturday night

Mass with family the evening before. I was surprised and pleased by his commitment to worship. In that way, he was different from other boys I had known.

By the time the two of us shared prom and graduation together, he wanted me to be his "steady girl."

I had to say "No."

At eighteen-years-old, I couldn't go steady with someone long distance. From our many conversations about family and relationships, I knew my local boy considered a steady relationship as a precursor to marriage. Roy and I hadn't first looked at each other over cafeteria spaghetti when the December letter arrived, informing me of early acceptance to Baylor University. Waco, Texas, was the closest thing to another hometown, with loving grandparents there, even if they did always grapple with my name. Mamoo, Dad, and several cousins before me had cheered the Green and the Gold. Upholding family tradition, comfortable knowing what to expect of the small Texas town blossoming into a city, I was excited to be a "Baylor Bear."

Not wanting to break Roy's heart, I asked that we both give each other freedom to date while apart. I promised I would stay in touch with him as my friend. I needed time to grow outside of my chaotic home, and a pause in our relationship, to hold him at arms-length to be certain he wasn't rushing me.

While we were apart, I dated a little, attending concerts, plays, and Homecoming, with no interest in sparking romantic relationships. I played tennis with a boy from Dayton, Ohio, but felt no "love" in the game. One evening, he lingered on the steps of Allen Hall, with that longing in his eye that said, "I might kiss you if we keep standing here."

Knowing the building matron kept her eye on male

students entering the freshmen girls' dorm, I steered him past her front desk into the large open parlor. There, I summoned the courage to tell him I was writing to a guy back home.

"I still care for him." I surprised myself by saying it aloud. "I don't want you to think I'm toying with you. . . but I'd still like us to play tennis."

He let me go gently and soon. I went back to the courts to play with whomever was slamming balls against a backboard. I had no regrets.

It was the Age of Aquarius. Roy attended Chaminade, a small Catholic institution near University of Hawaii, and played drums in a hippie rock band destined to go nowhere. I flipped through a handful of action shots he'd sent of the group. Fearing he looked too much like the "establishment" so reviled by the "groovy" generation, he had given up his military-style haircut and let his curls grow down over his collar. And he looked so much older with that first mustache. But his fellow musicians looked like the cast of Broadway musical *Hair,* sporting untamed, bushy locks, and beards resembling nests for wild things. Roy filled our time apart with classes and rehearsals. He was not dating anyone, happy to spend his free time keeping the beat for the band.

Across the miles, we shared our affection for the new rock group, The Eagles, and music of Neil Diamond, John Denver, and Carole King. We sweated together through the radio broadcast of the Selective Service Lottery for draft into the Vietnam war (his birthday was well beyond the fateful number) and exchanged increasingly mushy love letters. When a surprise shipment of tropical flowers from Honolulu to Waco landed on the dorm matron's front desk perch, my roommates nearly lost their minds.

"Ooh, Girl! . . .You have *got* to go back to that guy! . . . This is serious!"

The bouquet was bright red anthuriums, with heart-shaped blossoms (leaves) similar to a candleholder, surrounding a long yellowish-white spadix, standing erect from the center of the leaf. My roomies teased me about the rather phallic flowers until they faded. But what captured my eye was the cluster of crimson hearts. In the spirit of aloha, my high school sweetheart was pulling me back to him.

Although Baylor offered academic excellence and entertaining campus life, I decided that I would return home after completing my freshman year, and transfer to University of Hawaii. Dad accepted my terms, that although I would be coming back in Hawaii, I needed to live away from home. He may have been relieved that he would pay in-state tuition versus private college rates. At Christmas break, Roy presented me with a "promise ring," to be followed the next summer by a larger diamond. I completed my year at Baylor, thanked my Waco family for helping me feel at home, and hugged my roomies good-bye. Though our bonds were not strong, we shared a rite of passage in that first college year. I am confident that were our paths to cross, we would enjoy an evening of wine and memories of screaming "Sic 'em Bears!" at football games and sporting our "Freshmen Slime (ball)-caps," in and out of Allen Hall, deep in the heart of Texas.

Two flights and about nine hours later, I was back in summer gale-force winds under my roof at home in Hawaii. I clung to Roy as my anchor. Though not usually united on any subject, my parents allied to protest to our engagement, as they prepared to move to England for another of Dad's job transfers. My father promised to cover my expenses if I would at least complete college before getting married. Roy and I had no idea how hard a three year engagement could be. Had we had money to support ourselves, we wouldn't have waited.

§§§

Roy earnestly pursued a career with the Air Force R.O.T.C., a candidate for pilot training upon graduation, and I was a theatre major, dreaming of an acting or teaching career. Yet as I pondered a prospective life as a military wife, traveling from one assignment to the other, probably with children in tow, I began to see a bend in the road of my ambition. That bend turned into a sharp curve in the fall of my junior year.

In front of the entire class, the professor critiqued a final exam scene I had directed and rehearsed with several other actors.

"You haven't demonstrated even some of the basics . . ." he complained. "I don't know what you've learned here. . . You demonstrate no creative instincts!"

Or something to that effect. His exact words were lost in the heart-pounding throbbing I could feel behind my eyes, lowered in shame. The thumping moved to my ears and I stood alone on the stage, watching his mouth, twisting into a sneer. Was he really telling me I was hopeless at what I loved most? I had performed in a University musical mainstage production and taken a number of acting classes with this man. During prior coursework, I'd received helpful and constructive criticism, always a mix of praise and suggestions for improvement. This was a surprise full-frontal attack.

Fleeing the theatre that morning, gasping through flooding tears, I hadn't yet acquired the worldly experience to process what had happened over the previous two semesters. Years of maturity helped me piece together the puzzled memories and realize the professor's assault was personal.

At twenty and a bride-to-be, I had been oblivious to his motives. I'd brushed aside with light-hearted humor, the prof's subtle and sometimes suggestive comments. I thought he was just cracking dirty jokes—typical backstage banter. The professor was "an old guy" (probably in his forties, ha!). A woman young enough to have been his daughter waited for him at the end of rehearsals and would circle her arm around his waist, as they walked away from the theatre. I assumed she had been a former student. My interest in him? None.

Once I visited his office to drop off a paper, and he told me to sit awhile, not to rush off. I had other things to do. When I told him Roy and I were headed to a concert featuring popular rock group *Bread,* he asked what they sang. Politely, I rattled off song titles: "Baby, I'm-a Want You," and "I'd Like to Make it With You." Even today I cannot forget his eyes traveling over me and his leering response: "Yeah. That sounds good."

Further, when I turned down his suggestion to audition for a female lead with a sexually charged scene in an upcoming play, he flattered me into the show as Student Director/Stage Manager. Once, he sent me climbing into a backstage loft for some small props and followed me. He wasn't there to offer help; instead, he stood below, one hand in his jeans pocket, watching me ascend and descend the ladder. I had wondered why he just stood there looking at me.

The final "rebuff" before the public humiliation in class, occurred at the cast party after the show, when Roy and I refused offers to smoke marijuana and skinny dip in the hosts' pool. It wasn't our scene. Party-poopers, we left early. I found myself cast in the role of a prim "social misfit" amid my theatre peers. Worse yet, Roy's scholarship and prospects for a military career could evaporate if he were merely present in a group busted for smoking pot. Looking back, it was from that night on, that my professor had seemed aloof.

I fled the building that exam day, staggered by his vicious critique. Only a handful of professors ran the theatre program. How would I be able to audition for future productions, without prejudice against me? I knew then I could not continue a major in theatre.

Of all my desires then, I most wanted to marry Roy, have a family, and head for adventures in the Air Force's "wild blue yonder." What had I been thinking with my theatre aspirations? How could I devote my life to becoming a professional actress, teach drama, and be a military spouse at the same time? Slow came the dawning. I wasn't limited to a major in theatre. And I could decide to reject one instructor's low opinion of my potential. As a lover of literature and writing, I realized I could earn a Language Arts Education degree, with enough hours in my drama and speech courses to round out my options. Inspired by my favorite middle and high school English and drama teachers, along with brilliant professors in literature, writing and public speaking, I could embark on a teaching career that I could carry around the world. As a bonus, my children and I would have summers (and snow days) together. Also, I could include them in after-school rehearsals and set building on weekends. In time, they would become theatre-lovers and unofficial drama mascots, crafting props, or splashing paint on canvas.

And this was our life. Home was wherever their Daddy hung his Air Force blue cap. Ours was a constant rotation of moving into new spaces, pulling off the packing tape, and opening box upon box, making each house our home.

We adopted new schools, jobs, and friends, and then detached ourselves, as though pulling our own tape up, sometimes painfully, like yanking off band-aids. Then we healed — and repeated the process with the next assignment. My youth had prepared me for a military wife's need for adaptability; but the frequent arrivals and departures forced our children to learn to let go of the familiar, braving each transfer, with a willing (albeit, not always uncomplaining) spirit. Before newfound friendships and brief bonds formed, there was this foundation: they always had one another as buddies through every trial. From place to place, they also had the balm of being surrounded by their familiar belongings. But now, after Andrew, the survival of their belongings was questionable. We could only reassure them that in and out of every upheaval, they had us.

Does a Home Have a Soul?

*God has promised to supply all our needs. What we don't
have now, we don't need now.*

~ Elisabeth Elliot, *The Path of Loneliness*

Homestead, August 27, 1992

When we stopped along the curb of our street, both
of us bounded out and into each other's arms. Wearing
his battle dress uniform, dark circles under his eyes, Roy
embraced me hard, his cheeks scratchy and coarse. I didn't
care. I'd been aching to hold him. I'm sure we said some
affectionate words, but we needed to get to work. Only a
few daylight hours were left before the base curfew.

"You have the camera, hon?" he asked.

"Got it. Boots, helmets, rake, gloves. In the back seat."

We donned our gear. I stopped for a moment and touched
his arm as he started leading me around the carport to the
back of the house.

"Oh no. Look at Will's house!"

The man who had first alerted us of Andrew's bull's-eye
on our backyard would find his home under a collapsed
roof. The new nurse next door, whose unpacked household
goods were now in sodden cardboard, would be unable to
enter her house. A ring of yellow police tape warned the
structure was unstable. We were both sad for our neighbors
and grateful for our stubborn roof.

We reflexively tried the carport entry door to the house.

Still locked. Both of us found it absurd and funny. I stopped laughing as we walked toward the backyard.

Deep breath.

Exterior walls looked bruised, and a trash heap of tree limbs, loose boards, and foam insulation leaned against the house. Where there had been an enclosed patio with wood walls and a set of sliding glass doors into the family room, there was now only a concrete slab. Before us, our entryway was a dark, gaping hole, a mouth stretched wide in horror, like Munch's famous portrait, *The Scream.*

Where to begin? A knot tightened in my gut and up popped an impulse to bolt back to the car, never to return. But this silent ruin held our family's artifacts. Time to excavate relics of our married years, and a few precious childhood souvenirs. Curiosity rising, we realized we had to start somewhere, anywhere.

Roy held the rake in hand and pulled a piece of hanging aluminum door frame out of my path as I steadied the VHS video camera, roughly the size of a shoebox on my shoulder, and pulled it up to my eye.

"Careful," he said. Our entry point had been our informal dining area/family room, crowded with rattan furniture from three years in Italy.

"Can you believe this?!" Roy pointed to an orange plastic chair on top of the heap. Not ours.

I waded slowly, like a heron, raising each leg and easing it down as though to avoid making ripples across a swamp. Almost knee-deep, we sloshed through a morass of chunks of dry wall and crumpled sliding door glass, held together by reflective window film, asphalt roof shingles, branches, and scattered papers.

A random memory flashed through my mind: I recalled how Hemingway once described a battlefield strewn with the dead and their hundreds of papers blowing everywhere—letters, journals, books, and military orders. Now, peering through my camera lens, I had my first look at our "battlefield," everything splattered with grass, gleaming splinters, and black flecks, that we soon identified as exploded bits of tarry roofing paper, blown over and embedded in everything, like dark confetti.

When I later listened to my narration on the video, it sounded silly, feebly desperate for comic relief: "What a mess! I left this place clean."

Even now, how can I describe the smell? Perhaps like a mix of mildew with spoiled meat, rotting eggs, and over-ripe vegetables, simmering in the summer heat for a week.

I pushed away the revulsion and sloshed toward the kitchen. Growing numb, I began to eye our nest with the objectivity of a detective. We watched for jagged shards. Under our rubber soles were jars of grape jelly, mayonnaise, relish, and a carton of eggs flung into the formal dining area. Several eggs were still sitting in the carton, while others left a trail of broken shells scattered around the room.

"Look at that!" Roy said. "The doors were just blown open!" What mammoth force was this, that not only tore open windows and doors, but sealed refrigerators as well?

Yet the cereal bowls were still in the sink. There they sat, filled with murky water and surrounded by odds and ends that had swirled through the kitchen to the percussion of cupboard doors swinging and banging, now hanging from their hinges.

The combined living and dining area, once carpeted in sky blue, squished grey under our feet. Our large solid wood china hutch, lovingly called "the widow-maker" by a friend who once grunted and groaned to help Roy move it, first appeared untouched, as though the outgoing gale bypassed its glass doors. However, we would have to act fast to get to the wedding china out of the bottom cabinets, already swelling from moisture. Everything upholstered was wet and studded with slivers of glass. A bentwood rocking chair, my once peaceful place for nursing each of my babies, was going straight to the trailer. We agreed it was worth refinishing.

Over the dining room table, a wilting bouquet of birthday balloons from Kris's party still hung from the chandelier. . . evidence of the last breath of life in our home before the onslaught.

Every instinct said, "Don't touch anything!" But we had to touch, sometimes dig, in the muck. Along the hallway leading from the living room and foyer to the bedrooms, we found what was left of the row of old family photographs, affectionately named the "Rogues' Gallery." Most had fallen from the wall. Sepia images of our grandparents in bridal attire, a color enlargement of an irreplaceable candid taken on our wedding day, my mother's twenty-year old forties-film-star face, all soggy against the cracked glass of their frames. We picked up a few that appeared to only be wet along the edges and dropped others back onto the heap.

"We can get some of these redone," I murmured.

Roy's voice broke, "I hope."

I couldn't think of anything else to say to comfort him.

Debris was less deep as we moved into the hallway toward our bedrooms. Our master ceiling had a gaping hole, daylight winking through space in the roof. Just missing the end of our bed, a four-foot chunk of ceiling had dropped to the floor in the center of the room.

Everything we had placed on the mattress was still wrapped in plastic and was dry. Although we had removed some essential items–a couple of changes of clothes, jewelry, grooming and travel supplies from Roy's armoire and my dresser when we evacuated, it didn't take long for them to seal shut. For several years after, we would look for casual clothes–a souvenir theme park tee-shirt, a favorite sweater or comfortable pair of shorts–all remained entombed in that furniture. But the contents of our closet were salvageable and were debris-free. We hadn't lost it all.

From room to room, we would repeat a kind of song — lament and praise, all in one: "Oh, *that* didn't make it / Oh, good, *that* can go with us."

I caught my breath as I looked at Jimmy's room. Window glass covered his twin beds. The following day of salvaging, stuffing what toys I could into a box, I could not keep from glancing at those beds. What if evacuation hadn't been mandatory? I couldn't think about it.

One look down the hallway to the girls' bedrooms and we realized two startling facts: storm surge had blasted through Seana's bedroom window and rushed through to the next logical opening, our master bedroom, leaving up the wall, a six-foot high trail of flotsam and jetsam, such as one sees along a seashore. We could trace the water line, mixed with grass and other detritus. In the oft-recommended hallway "refuge" in a Florida home during storms, we might have been injured or killed had we not evacuated. We both made a mental note: better to dive into an interior closet or bathroom.

Seana's room had been hit the hardest. After ripping through her window and spinning her metal blinds into a weird spiky corkscrew, the surge ruined almost all her belongings. My heart grieved to see her bookshelf soaked. Drowned were the "old friends" I had brought to my children from my own childhood: Grimm's and Anderson's fairy tales, Robert Louis Stevenson's *A Child's Garden of Verses*, Dr. Seuss favorites. Her bed, like that of her little brother, was a field of glass. The closet had been thrown open; the remains of her shattered window covered her clothes, leaving none salvageable. Above the top shelf, an updraft had sucked almost all of a folded comforter into the attic crawl space. Reaching down like a small hand, a shred of peach-tinted corner was all we could see.

The greatest surprise was Krissie's room. A mattress-sized piece of sheet metal had wedged between a tree and her window. Her space appeared as she had left it, except for the damp floor. Her unfortunate goldfish was struggling in the murky bowl, hemorrhagic spots riddling his body. Pitifully, we dropped a pinch of food for him and added a little water from the bathtub. By the end of our salvaging days, he was gone. Some of my numbness trickled away at the thought of losing even so small a member of our family. I chided myself: Who cries for a goldfish?

At the end of that first day of recovery, we were forced to stop for respite from the 90-plus degree heat and heavy humidity. Having secured most of the items on the short lists of my children—the toy cars, ballet slippers, journals, and contact lenses—and more than excavating anything else from the house, I wanted to flee the fetid atmosphere.

Roy's temporary shelter, the remains of the base Conference Center near the house, had some broken windows, but a generator pumping air conditioning into the damp rooms. With a usable bathroom, I welcomed a rinse in cool water and soap. Even if I had to put the same clothes back on, I hoped I had scrubbed the stink of the house from my skin. I kissed my weary "warrior" good-bye and headed back to the old home.

Dad was waiting for me and the latest news from Roy and the base. Exhausted, out of words, I showed him the videotape of those first moments in the house. He murmured his typical "Dad-isms:" *Oh, my Lord . . . Just look at that! . . . My Lord!* And he made his dismayed "tsk-

tsk" sound with his tongue behind his front teeth when he'd run out of words.

He had set up a t.v. tray, and served up grilled corned beef hash, green beans, and half-smiles of sliced peaches. My father attempted to love and console me with the offer of this food from his hands, but I could not unknot my throat. He coaxed me to eat for strength and tenderly salted the meal with only a pinch of small talk. Perhaps he sensed that I was crumbling under the weight of the day's enormity?

In the soothing light of a hurricane lamp, my father sat close by, and at last, a few tired tears mingled with the sweat on my face. My mother, tucked into her bedroom sanctuary, never came out that evening to join us.

When power is out on an August night in Miami, the light fades well after 8 p.m., and there is a boredom that settles in when only a flickering lantern can light up a book or card game. I said my "good nights" to my parents, staggered to the guest room, and shed all but my dingy tee shirt before crawling into bed.

Sleep was inversely proportional to my fatigue. For a long time, I lay there, windows open, praying for a breeze. While I was trying to listen for God's reassurance that He was near, suddenly, I heard a POP! POP-POP! Sound is a deceiver in darkness, but it sounded like gunshots from the property a half-acre behind us. I panicked. I had already seen warning signs as I'd traveled: "LOOTERS WILL BE SHOT!" Definitely pistol-shots. Was someone trying to steal our neighbor's provisions?

Questions tripped one over the other, as I tensed in the damp sheets. What if someone tried to break into this house? Would Dad be prepared to shoot? I would be no help. Longing for daylight, I prayed for safety again, as I had the night of the hurricane. Eventually, the Lord's promise of "peace beyond understanding" poured over me, and I slept.

The next day, our base house was robbed. While we paused in the shade of the conference center, gobbling down peanut butter sandwiches and cookies Dad had bagged for us, looters took two table-top speakers and the computer from inside the house, and from the garage shed, the lawn mower and pair of snow skis. We later learned these thieves were people authorized to be on base. Brothers-in-arms stealing from their own!

Roy cursed but took comfort that the salty storm surge had probably already stolen from the robbers any satisfaction of using their electronic loot.

Outraged that someone would kick us while we were down, we later considered how irresistible it must have been for the greedy. Without walls and windows, homes were cracked open, like giant treasure chests. Whatever bits and pieces were left, were there for our salvaging, for their scavenging.

But no one could steal the soul of our home. That was tucked inside each of us.

§§§

I returned the U-Haul back to Riverview the next day, stowed our load in Carol's garage and returned with her and with packing supplies in Ralph's pick-up truck for the next load. She helped us for the next two days, packing dishes, glassware, and breakables from the hutch. I was surprised by my increasing revulsion at re-entering my home. Violated, it no longer felt like ours anymore. The literal darkness within those walls swamped me in sorrow. Wasn't this supposed to provide relief, gathering some of our worldly goods?

Each trip into the carport, the only shady spot left in the hot yard, we staged small tables, clothes, shoes, toys, and tools. We wrapped breakables in towels and sheets when we ran out of paper. My mind chided, "It's just stuff." But my heart struggled with picking and choosing what could be repaired or safely packed.

Each time I walked out of the stinking shell of what had been a comfortable nest, I willed myself back inside. Some moments the three of us would rush outside, gasping for clean air. Fighting dehydration, we gulped warm water from gallon jugs, then poured a little on our hands and faces.

One of Roy's co-workers stopped in our driveway as we wedged the last of our salvage into the truck.

"Can you believe this, Roy?" he said. We exchanged sweaty hugs with him and his wife.

She began to moan. "I've lost so many antiques. Things that have been in my family for over a hundred years. I'm just sick." She began detailing her list of lost heirlooms.

Maybe it was the swelter. Had my empathy evaporated in the heat? Perhaps my nerve ends were singed by the smell of decay in my nose, or I was sore from surrendering my own death-grip on pictures and souvenirs and amulets of memory to the muck inside. I had no words for her. I wanted to say, "You are alive and unhurt. What does all this stuff really matter anyway?"

But I kept my jaws clamped tight. Maybe I nodded my head as she spoke. It was the best I could do. And we had some bottled water left. We could offer them that.

When do we make that turn—whether as a gentle bend in our journey or a sudden curve—that begins to raise us from the depths of grieving lost things? Revelation dawns: not a single thing is going where we are headed. Cliches abound: "No pockets in shrouds; no U-Haul behind the hearse."

That hellish afternoon we were still learning to trust the

One we claimed as Savior. It was going to be years before we took to heart Jesus's teaching to His disciples:

"Fear not, little flock, for it is your Father's good pleasure to give you the kingdom. Sell your possessions and give to the needy. Provide yourselves with moneybags that do not grow old, with a treasure in the heavens that does not fail, where no thief approaches and no moth destroys. For where your treasure is, there will your heart be also." [1]

But trusting in divine advice and surrendering our earthly treasure may take a lifetime. We filled the bed of that truck.

As Roy and I parted at dusk, reuniting our family dogged my thoughts. Neither of us knew when he would be officially finished with the recovery of the base but hoped it would be soon. As we drove toward the main gate, I was too spent to look back at the house or the remains of Homestead Air Force Base. I believed I would never see them again.

By next morning light, I hugged my parents goodbye, feeling confident they were surrounded by attentive neighbors. All of them would all have to wait seventeen days for the simple joys of glowing light bulbs, television, refrigeration, and fresh meals cooked in the oven.

Even for sisters, our drive back to Riverview was quiet. Our minds still struggled to process the events of the week. Missing was my chirpy road companion, Foofer. His simple life was already restored to normal. I felt hollowed out, an empty vessel. Soon, I would understand that was exactly what God had planned for me. So cluttered was my life with self-sufficiency and other idols, I didn't realize I needed to make room for His Spirit to dwell — not dormant, but afire inside me.

But on that four-hour trip back to Riverview, I wasn't

thinking about faith or future plans or anything but holding my children close. There was treasure, indeed.

On Breathing, Before a Consideration of Coincidence

For I know the plans I have for you declares the Lord, plans for welfare and not for evil, to give you a future and a hope.

~ Jeremiah 29:11

Riverview, Mid-October 1992

Tampa's stores began filling with fall regalia, pumpkin spice potpourri, and Halloween costumes. At last, Roy was on his way to Riverview. He had orders for our move. With cheers and whoops, we rushed out of the house to greet him as he pulled into Carol and Ralph's cypress mulch driveway. After three weeks of living in combat zone-monsoon conditions, reeking in unwashed uniforms, and simmering in his damp conference center room, he came "home" to us, sick.

What seemed like a bad cough and cold was diagnosed as walking pneumonia. Roy desperately needed an "R and R," military term for rest and recuperation. But as the active-duty member of our family, he had to sign in at MacDill Air Force Base in Tampa for his paycheck. One errand led to another; we tried to temper our eagerness to begin replacing household necessities with naps and relaxed evenings of television and movies. Yet good food, rest in a safe, comfortable bed, and plenty of familial affection were not getting results.

Still running on "a drained tank," after two weeks on Erythromycin, he renewed his prescription. All the comforts of my sister's home could not prevent a near catastrophe.

One evening, his face long and haggard, Roy said, "I'm going to bed," and coughed his way down the hall. Within a few minutes, Carol strode up the same hallway and found me in the kitchen.

"Hey, Roy's not sounding good back there. He's wheezing pretty hard."

I checked on him and heard labored breaths.

" Roy," I said. His eyes were closed. "Honey, I think you might need to go to the hospital."

His voice was hushed, weak. "Naw, I just need sleep."

"Have you taken your meds tonight?"

"Yeah," he wheezed. "I'm just having trouble catching my breath."

Carol and I shared a worried look and I headed for the phone. MacDill, with our designated medical facility, was situated at the far side of Tampa, forty-five minutes away. I called the ER anyway.

After I described the symptoms, the technician on phone duty recited the regulations:

"You can bring him in ma'am, but I can't tell you whether or not you should. We can't make that determination over the phone. If you think he needs to be seen, you should take him to the closest emergency room."

"Let's GO!" I said, grabbing my purse and taking no argument from my mildly protesting husband. He wasn't the only one entitled to dispense orders.

Carol volunteered to stay with the children, as Ralph was nominated "ambulance driver." Off we went to Brandon Hospital, the closest emergency room to their house.

The trip seemed interminable, although now that I live in the area, I find it wasn't more than a fifteen-minute drive. Roy rested in the backseat, each breath a faint whistle. I wanted to take the wheel and fly to the ER. Ralph, a steady and patient man, made some small talk to calm me, but I only listened to the raspy respiration behind my seat. He dropped us off in the ambulance lane and left to park the car. By the time he returned to the reception area, orderlies had whisked Roy into a treatment area, with me, flying behind him, as soon as I had produced an i.d. card, signed this acknowledgment and that authorization, promising to foot the bill if Uncle Sam didn't.

With an oxygen mask on his face and an intravenous needle in his arm, patient "Jardin, R." had just received a shot of epinephrine.

"He was going into anaphylactic shock," the attending physician explained. "Looks like a reaction to the E-mycin." Then the unexpected chuckle: "When you go to the front of the line before the Saturday night gunshot victim, you know you've got an issue."

I let that drip into my system. An issue. . . of life and breath. . . Breathers before bleeders. A few more minutes of Roy's gasping for oxygen, and I would have been a homeless widow, pressing against my heart a triangular-folded flag and three young children.

The epinephrine did its magic and Roy began to breathe regularly. The amiable doctor changed his prescription and discharged his patient with instructions to take care of the pneumonia with lots of rest. What irony that my husband hadn't entered the danger zone until the second two-weeks on the Erythromycin!

As his strength returned, my Roy's organizational instincts kicked in and he asked me to find the phone number of the realtor in Woodbridge, Virginia. It was time to officially find a house within commuting distance of Washington D.C. Wouldn't the agent be surprised to hear from us! While on vacation, we had taken a preliminary peek around the area we expected to relocate to with Roy's next military assignment. We had met the realtor two weeks before Hurricane Andrew destroyed my "Day Planner." June of 1993 had been marked for "Move to Pentagon."

§§§

No hurricane was yet on anyone's summer of '92 radar when we spent some early August days with lifelong friends, Diane and Richard Scott, and their only daughter Jennifer Leilani. We were celebrating our news of a second move to Virginia. Four years before, we had been blessed to live close to the Scotts, while Roy was stationed at Langley Air Force Base, near the small tidewater town of Poquoson. We would scoot back and forth across the James River Bridge for get-togethers, relaxing by the banks of the river on a strip of beach behind their house. Krissie and Jennifer were two years apart and played together, while Seana and Jimmy learned the basics of fishing for striped bass and croaker with "Uncle" Richard." "Auntie" Diane's kitchen was a fragrant, welcome place for Southern-style over-indulgence. Our only complaints were full bellies and the aches and pains of nonstop merriment. Richard's comical facial expressions and "put-on's" could work Roy into almost uncontrolled laughter.

Richard once caused a scene in Miami's International Airport when the Scott family wrapped up a visit with us in our assignment to Homestead. Roy, ever his partner in crime, pulled out the video camera and signaled "action." There our friend stood, exclaiming as the crowd moved around him like water around a rock.

"I can't believe it!" His eyes wide, he declared in his best stage projection, "I come to vacation in Florida and I win the lotto!" Several travelers paused and stared.

"Richard!" Diane said, in mock disapproval. Then she began laughing, as we all did, his monologue continuing:

"I don't know what I'll do with all that money. Can you believe it, the Florida Lotto!"

He had acted a similar charade once on a Virginia ski trip. Close to the lodge, a shelf of trophies awaited winners of a competition later that day. Richard stood alongside the awards, while Roy struggled to steady the video camera.

"I'm so honored," he said, again with a curious audience tromping by in the snow, skies resting on their shoulders. "I didn't think I would place, but to win here today. . ." And on he would roll, gleeful that he could bamboozle the crowd—and keep all of us entertained.

Diane and I had been friends since college, but Roy's and Richard's deepening bond was a delightful development. At the outset, could Diane and I ever have imagined that our men with such different experiences would become buddies?

In 1973, our mutual college advisor, the late Julie Alm, was the unknowing casting director in a drama that continues to play out in our lives, running now for over four decades. She recognized that Diane and I shared some of the same passion for teaching literature and theatre, and suggested we try to find one another. She was certain that we would probably be "kindred spirits."

Kindred, indeed!

We were destined to (almost literally) run into one another on a sunny island morning at University of Hawaii's Manoa campus. Coming around two portable classrooms, schedules in hand, we had to stop short to avoid a head-on crash. Fortunately, we were on foot. Some brief polite words flew between us, both laughing the way people do in a "Whoops!" without casualties. We were hunting for a classroom, I believe, when we realized we were in the same academic pursuit.

Two questions merged our two lives:

"Are you Bronwyn?" she asked.

"Are you Diane?" I smiled back, somehow already knowing.

We still cheer our advisor's wise instincts. Neither of us believe our meeting was accidental. On a large sprawling state university with multiple campuses, two "mainland girls," stepped into one another's paths, and began traveling a lifelong journey together.

Our men were headed in opposite directions. She was married to Richard, her high school sweetheart, a recovering wounded soldier, still entangled in memories of Vietnam; I was engaged to Roy, "chomping at the bit" to get into an Air Force cockpit. Richard was fighting to put the barbs of battle behind him, while my fiancé was anxious to be called to action. Diane wasn't sure their marriage would survive the post-traumatic stress, while I was dreaming about an island wedding. Through comedy and tragedy on our life stage, Diane grew to be like another sister; our men became as brothers.

Fast forward to 1992. As soon as we received word Roy was scheduled to move from Homestead to the Pentagon, we drove to Virginia for a quick late summer vacation and a celebratory toast. In less than a year, we would live three hours from our friends. In a gift of sweet generosity, Uncle Richard and Auntie Diane kept our children for a day while Roy and I took a quick trip to look at neighborhoods in Northern Virginia.

For no other reason than we liked the sound of a town named "Woodbridge," in Prince William County, we enlisted the help of a realtor. About twenty-two miles from

Roy's new "base," it was a small city and a community with plenty of amenities. Heading the opposite direction from D.C., Quantico Marine Corps Base was only a few miles away. For shopping and medical emergencies, we liked knowing a military installation was close to home.

We established a file of preferences with the realtor and were grateful for the windshield tour of neighborhoods and schools. He understood we couldn't seriously consider house options until the following summer. We assured him we would be in touch.

After Roy's salvaging work at Homestead and his breathless near – death experience, he suggested I tell our realtor, "We're coming a little sooner than expected."

So, our whim to look over the housing prospects for a transfer almost a year away turned out to be a time-saver and gift to our peace of mind. Roy and I had already designated a city, we just needed a new nest there.

One day, we would believe that returning to Virginia, again moving closer to our beloved friends, was no cosmic happenstance. True, it offered us opportunities for more frequent visits, day trips to famous Virginia landmarks, and Christmas and birthday celebrations together. But a time was coming when the Scotts would need us to be close.

We would declare that a Divine plan was surely in the works from before the first day Diane and I found ourselves at a fateful campus intersection on a tiny verdant dot in the largest ocean on the planet. Our lives, those of our husbands, and our children were all bound to intertwine. Our enduring friendship would make perfect sense in an imperfect and confounding world.

I don't believe in coincidences.

White Winds and Searching for the Star

*Oh, mightiest wind, wilt thou cease thy breathing in and
hold thy exhales?*

~ Richelle E. Goodrich, *Making Wishes*

Northern Virginia, late 1992

Only once in their father's career would the children see official PCS (permanent change of station) orders scribbled onto an Air Force form. Andrew had destroyed the Personnel Office computer responsible for generating the appropriate documents. Whether scrawled or typed, the orders directed us to begin our journey into the Pentagon years. At last, we could begin the end of the Homestead chapter.

For nine weeks, we had piled almost every corner of Carol and Ralph's home and garage with trappings old and new, and still managed to all remain friendly. Living in the home of two full-time teachers, along with Ralph's live-in mother and Taipan, the dog, Roy and I had often tried to offset the strain of five extra people, plus small pets, by grocery shopping, doing household chores, and having dinner ready when they came in from school.

They helped us load up a trailer large enough to accommodate the salvaged goods and several replacement

131

items purchased as we awaited the orders to move. Had we not spent numerous vacations together, we might have been weepy, but now, it felt like another Air Force transfer. We knew, as always, we would reunite in our new home, or theirs. Next time, though, we would arrive without the U-Haul.

The children's first quarter of school was behind them. Realizing it was a tough assignment for displaced kids who knew they were short-timers, we'd counseled them, explaining despite our upheaval, their Virginia teachers would want to see evidence of schooling while in Florida. "Just jump in and give it all the gusto you can muster," we had advised. They each carried reports proving they'd made a good start. I marveled at their resiliency and determination to press on. How had they learned to be so brave?

§§§

Optimism bubbled up afresh like the Florida cumulus puffs we left in our wake. Our children were now old enough not to whine *ad nauseum* for potty-stops, a fast-food drink, or permission to leave a sibling at the next gas station. Because they could all play the License-Plate Game, and rotate positions between our two cars each time we stopped to re-fuel, we no longer had to threaten to take their heads like the Three Stooges and "knock 'em together" for misbehaving in the back seat. Had we not been bifurcated throughout the trip and hauling a trailer, it might have felt like vacation again. Looking up the road north through the Georgia and South Carolina pines and the colorful wildflowers gracing the medians of I-95 through North Carolina, we rejoiced. Even temporary living in guest quarters at Ft. Belvoir, just south of Washington D.C. filled us with hopeful anticipation of moving into our new house after a short wait.

By late fall, we were settling into our new home in Woodbridge. It had been the last house we considered. Heading back to the realtor's office, we were disappointed in houses in our price range. We feared we were going to have to explore areas further away from the Pentagon.

Then the agent spotted an Open House sign in an attractive subdivision. "What do you think?" he asked. Clean streets, landscaped yards, well-loved homes.

"Let's check it out," Roy said. It was a five-year-old gem, in almost perfect condition, with a weeping willow and Bradford pear trees all around. The yard was spacious enough we would not hear the neighbors' playlist, and the tan-brick-faced house with russet shutters sat up on a slight hill. Four bedrooms, full basement, and a small privacy-fenced backyard. Almost perfect. But we'd nearly missed it because it didn't match the criteria on my wish-list.

No front porch. The architectural lines of the colonial saltbox design featured a "stoop entry." To me, it looked like something was missing. My thought: "Who chopped off the front of the house?!"

Wasn't covered space around the front door essential? This South Florida girl grew up on porches . . . ours and those of all my relatives. Mamoo and Bapoo's Waco porch was a haven for terrorized horned toads scampering from me, a pajama-clad tomboy kid hunting them down barefoot-early, before breakfast. The Tucker porch in North Miami was hugged on all sides by periwinkles. I'd picked them to give my wheelchair bound Mamaa. Aunts and uncles, everyone of any importance in my life, had some kind of shady space with swings or rockers or plants around the entry, and we were considering a home without this crucial element?

Anxious to have a home again, I agreed to sacrifice tradition. No problem, until the heavy, drifting, Virginia snows came each winter. We sometimes opened the front door to a frozen white wall. I *knew* porches existed for good reason!

As the last fading cascade of autumn leaves skittered down the street and squealing children raked and leapt into their neat piles, the couple next door told us we were known as "the family that survived Hurricane Andrew." If that was celebrity, I'd not choose it again. Our emotional storm still raging, Roy and I repeated our story to anyone who asked. Riddled with chills or shaking, our "talk therapy" helped us process the catastrophe. However, we were still skittish.

In January, when a nor'easter named the "White Hurricane of '93" barreled up the east coast toward Washington D.C., we almost panicked.

"NO!" I cried, watching the nightly news. "We can't do another hurricane!"

We didn't have a choice. Incredulous, securing all emergency items for power outage, including of course, the "king of essentials," toilet paper, we braced for a big blow. Our second windstorm in fewer than five months. With icy hurricane force winds, our first mid-Atlantic storm roared outside while we cringed in front of a late-night log fire.

Clunk! BOOM-BOOM-Clatter-CRASH!

I almost dove under the couch, as Roy sprang up to peer into darkness outside. Had we survived Andrew, only to be crushed in our new home?

Thankfully, we had power and an outside light. "It's a big piece of something on the deck," he said. I jumped up from the couch and stood at his side, trying to figure out what we were seeing.

"Oh, my gosh," he continued. "I think it's the chimney cap."

And so it was, and we sustained no other damage except

for a few more frayed nerves. We murmured a quick prayer: "Thank you, O God, for protecting us from the wind. Again."

Even when your heart and mind tell you, "This is good. I am a survivor. I'm given a chance to begin again," trauma has a way of lying in wait. It hides in dark corners of a new house. It startles. It curls around sagging shoulders and tightens the throat, when a phrase, a photo, or a phone call takes you back into the storm. My wish to kick it into the dust behind us was not yet granted.

For the first few months, when wind moaned outside, I sometimes sprang from bed, looked out windows, checked my sleeping children, and paced around the house. Downstairs I would go, without a destination, with more peering out into noisy darkness. Knowing I needed my sleep, I would coax myself back up the stairs and into the bed. Years tumbled by before I didn't tense at a wintry howl or a sudden gust on a tempestuous summer night.

Possibly because of post-traumatic anxiety, mixed with the challenges and distractions of settling our family into our new environment, I didn't pause to ponder why I wasn't trusting God to continue caring for us. My prayer-life was erratic, Bible reading rare and random. But with a roof intact, and most boxes unpacked, Roy and I next focused on finding a church home.

Selecting a suitable church community and congregation was not a "once and done." Each move meant another search. With so many years of rote worship and checking all the sacrament squares for each child: First Confession, Communion, Confirmation … and rotating from one base chapel to another, we weren't even sure what we were seeking. Of one thing we were both positive: The King of kings, our comforting Heavenly Father, who hovered over us as distant lightning heralded Andrew's western departure, deserved a throne room in our hearts. But, as one family, we couldn't build it alone. We needed the fellowship of other believers.

§§§

Christmas was coming and never had we longed more for "Peace on Earth!" Our first attempt to attend a nearby church had worked for a couple of weeks, until we realized we had walked onto a battlefield: parishioners versus politician-priest. Too much steam under the steeple! With children between the ages of eleven and sixteen, we decided on the "Children's Mass," at another church. Its early hour would allow us to return home, enjoy our family tradition of opening a single mysterious package under the tree, and watch *It's a Wonderful Life* or *White Christmas* before settling down for the night.

The church was stuffed with families like an overflowing stocking. During a pre-Mass time of silent prayer and reflection on our knees, noise overwhelmed us. For a moment my mind flashed back to Miami a year before. Our little Jim had played a shepherd in the Holy Rosary School Christmas program, and at moments, bundled in sheets and burlap, he forgot he was tending his lambs, grinning and wiggling toward his watching family. Yet, when he sang carols, he was reverent and focused; we could hear his clear, beautiful voice.

The brief sweet memory was interrupted by more people pressing in, packing the pews around us. I almost gagged at the stewing aroma of peppermint, old-lady perfume, and a poopy diaper. More than anything, how our family longed for the heavenly essence of serenity and calm again!

The scene was helter-skelter. Surely, the priest expected the children to follow his homily with obedient attention. Roy and I exchanged an incredulous look. Pious and grave, the cleric used academic vocabulary soaring above the target audience's collective tousled heads. Four and five syllable words. Youngsters, probably already high on an afternoon (or week?) of sugarplums, roamed in the aisles. Parents attempted to absorb something meaningful from their parish leader, at the expense of keeping their children in their seats. Where was the children's Nativity play, or at least the Gospel presented in words simple enough to inspire a preschooler? What was wrong with "God came down as baby Jesus in a manger to bring love and peace to all the world?"

It never happened. At least, not in that service.

We were disappointed, so *done* with disorder and chaos. . . . Never mind the absence of a children's play, where was the reverence for the coming of the Christ Child? Where was the holy anticipation of one of the most important nights of the Church year? A few Christmas carols later, the irony of ending the service with "Silent Night" was palpable. As giddy youngsters danced on their toes, free at last from the confines of pews and kneelers, I was relieved the passing of candlelight among worshippers was reserved for adults at midnight Mass.

Fleeing from the church to our car, our family lamented that it was one of the worst worship experiences ever. As we pulled into the driveway, Roy gave me an order in his best military demeanor—and he was not one to bark orders at me unless it was a matter of life and limb.

"Find us a church this week. That was crazy. Totally unacceptable."

I hesitated. "I don't know where the nearest Catholic church is—the two we've been to are the only ones I know of nearby."

"Well, find us something. I don't have time to look. We're two strikes and almost out!"

We retreated into the warm quiet of our new home, to our familiar habits of Christmas Eve joy, sweetened with homemade iced butter cookies and hot chocolate. Jim laid two cookies on a plate for Santa, along with a can of Coke near the tree, even though we were all old enough now to know the Truth.

The Truth was God had indeed been generous and merciful this season. Before Andrew, the Christmas decoration boxes, mostly cardboard, spent eleven months a year in a self-storage unit in downtown Homestead. The business had hit-and-miss damage, and we were astounded to find the padlocked door to our unit held tight. The corrugated metal roof was dented into a "V" shape, which shunted the rainwater across the top of the unit, to the ground. Inside, almost everything was dry. Our stockings, ornaments my father's age, and homemade trinkets were almost all intact. The tree in our new living room comforted us with its piney perfume and the myriad of "survivors," each with its own story, nestled in the branches.

Still in our dressy best, we all reached for that one intriguing package from under the tree and satisfied our curiosity. Sensing this was going to be a "big Christmas," after losing so many of their belongings, the children were now breathless and took a few hours to settle down in anticipation of the coming morning. We knew Christ's birth was not about treasures on this earth, but we surprised them with new bikes, books, clock radios, and boomboxes, hoping to help them turn their attention away from all they'd physically lost at summer's end. None of us knew that night the true bounty awaiting us.

We almost hoped for a star to lead us to a place of worship. Roy and I continued the search-for-church conversation in bed. I took a gamble.

"I've seen a little church up a hill, a couple of blocks away—when I've been walking. But it's not Catholic. It's called 'All Saints.' I think it's Episcopalian — kind of 'Catholic-light?'" I paused.

I didn't think he would give in on this. I had been raised Protestant, converting to Catholicism before we married. Both sides of his family were Roman Catholic, without exception.

As we nestled down on our pillows, Roy sighed.

"I don't care. Check it out. That was the *worst* tonight. How could a priest give a Mass geared to kids and talk so far over their heads? No wonder it was so chaotic."

Relief washed over me. A Protestant church? Could it be possible? "I'll see what I can find out about the services," I told him. Then we exchanged a good-night kiss. "Merry Christmas, Santa," I whispered. "If the kids aren't still up, you better go eat those cookies and leave the empty Coke can."

"Oh yeah," he sighed, climbing off the bed. "And leave a few crumbs on the plate, right?"

"Right."

We had not left our few family traditions behind in the heap that was Homestead.

Encountering Splendor and Grief

Whoever does not know God hidden in suffering does not know God at all.

~ Martin Luther

Woodbridge, Winter 1992-1993

For my husband, it was a leap of faith. For all of us, it was a two-minute drive. In warmer weather, we could have walked from our home. On the first Sunday after Christmas, up the hill we went, five of us tumbling out of the station wagon in the All Saints Church parking lot.

Parishioners, many in families, led the way into the burnt sienna brick sanctuary. Smiling, they said, "Good Morning," and "Merry Christmas!" We'd hoped to maintain a low profile as visitors—what if we didn't like the place or the worship style? Afterward, we didn't want to be noticeable, possibly slinking away. Yet, each person we met was friendly, welcoming.

The service began and we slipped into a familiar rhythm of worship, reminiscent of Catholic Mass; I had a feeling we'd come to the right place. As we sang a Christmas hymn, the organ's triumphant chords reverberated around us. Sunlight cascaded through the tall casement windows, streaming down through stained glass panels, bathing the heads of the worshippers, almost as with haloes. Despite the church's name, I knew we were not "all saints." Was this what a heavenly manifestation of glory looks like—a splendor of souls radiating joy in their vocal praise? In this place, I thought, the Savior is truly exalted. If I were directing the scene cinematography for a film, a viewer might say, "This is cliché, over the top." I don't believe for one moment that what I remember is an exaggeration. It was illumination.

I nudged Roy and whispered, "Look at the light!" Surrounded by the shining faces of worshippers, I felt embraced. But these were not passive participants. I saw many arms raised, heads turned upward, hands opened, rather than folded in prayer. Nothing about it seemed false or forced, but devout and intimate.

I hang my head in shame to recall that I had once passed judgment against a fellow student for what I then deemed "showy" praise behavior in church. During my year at Baylor, I had a dorm-mate who came from a different Protestant denomination than the Baptist and Methodist majority. One Sunday, when an interdenominational gaggle of us attended the First Baptist Church in downtown Waco, I recall feeling uncomfortable as she stood at my side, striking several poses involving arms and hands lifted. What was *this*? She appeared devout, eyes closed, body engaged in praise and worship. My Methodist background suggested one showed reverence by remaining unnoticeable and motionless in church, except to turn the pages of the hymnal. "Why the show?" I wondered.

So put off by her demonstrative style, I distanced myself from her, thinking we probably would not become very good friends. Besides, I doubted her sincerity when she reacted with shock and horror at girls bragging of Friday night breakouts from the guarded suites of our dorm. In what kind of shelter had she been living? We were seventeen and eighteen years wise. Why so astounded by whispers of beer and weekend sex? I began to think of her as a "holier-than-thou, goody-goody." True hypocrisy because I, too, was mildly surprised by the brazen freshmen rule-breakers.

We never enjoyed a close bond, but whenever I picture her, she is standing beside me, hands and lips worshipping with unabashed fervor. How was it now, so many years later, I felt welcome and at home with a crowd who also checked self-consciousness at the church door and physically praised God with open arms?

Following the service, parishioners invited us to join them in an adjacent meeting room for refreshments and conversation. Our children recognized a couple of familiar faces from school, and Roy and I left assured that we would return the following Sunday.

We returned for three-and-a-half years of Sundays. Happily, we watched our children grow in the fertile soil provided there to raise up youth in the light of Christ-centered teaching. To this day, they remain friends with the husband-and-wife leaders who were shepherds to nourish our lambs, fresh from a spiritual wasteland.

Likewise, Roy and I immersed ourselves in the generous offerings of the church. We longed to better know this God who had brought us safely through the storm. With the church's proximity to home, we could easily participate in the choir and Sunday evening Bible studies. For the first time, we studied the Old and New Testaments, the whole Bible, cover-to-cover. Friendships blossomed and each week, we were eager to return, as our pastors challenged us to learn and live our faith.

One morning, while singing hymns, I realized my hands were rising from the sides of my body. Arms reaching toward Heaven, I wasn't ashamed of my supplication for healing. At last, I understood the irresistible urge to physically reach out to embrace the Spirit of God.

We had never come before the Almighty with such deep

hunger. Lingering images of Homestead's base chapel, splintered and collapsed in on itself, still haunted me. Before our home crumpled, we had often used church as a flimsy prop or an empty shell, where we brought brokenness we kept trying to repair on our own, while claiming to trust God. Then how we'd hurried to establish normalcy again for ourselves and our children! Rushing to replace everything we had lost, oblivious to the irony of making the first post-hurricane Christmas overabundant, racing to and fro to find and agree on a place of worship, we were still yearning.

§§§

As we restarted our family life in Woodbridge, we assumed our insurance payoff after the storm would offset the losses and help us put the hard memories behind us. Before our first overseas move to Italy in 1981, we had begun investing in "replacement-value" insurance to compensate us just in case our storage containers "jumped ship" into the middle of the Atlantic, or the moving van incinerated in a multi-vehicle pile-up on the interstate.

We visited our insurer's Tampa office not long after Roy had recovered from pneumonia. The insurance adjuster listened to our tale of woe and nodded in sympathy. His jaw then dropped, as Roy handed him a two-inch pile of printed paper: our household inventory. And for good measure, I tossed in the videotape of our base house, shot before and after.

"Wow!" said the adjuster. "You definitely were prepared."

The policy paid off. The first check had been written on-site at our insurer's makeshift office in a trailer at Homestead; the balance helped ease recovery shopping. Before we left Tampa, Carol had exclaimed, "It's kind of fun to get so much new stuff!" I'm sure I gave her a wild, demented look, as she quickly qualified: "But not because of going through a hurricane."

For the first time in our marriage, Roy and I watched rooms of new furniture roll in, on one truck after another. Our previous dwellings featured "military eclectic" interior design. As newlyweds, we'd completed our furnished one-bedroom apartment with a desk, a night table, two pressboard bookcases, and a waste basket. Our first piece of "nice" furniture was the salvaged nursing rocker, purchased to celebrate the day I heard Seana's tiny heart beating in my womb. As our family grew, a hodge-podge of used pieces donated by Mom and Dad helped us along. In time, we filled our home. Much of our décor was inlaid with memories of life in Italy and Turkey. We left behind most of those treasures, sodden and irreplaceable.

Now satisfied with the new furnishings, settling everyone into their new space, we threw ourselves into our respective work. I enjoyed time for homemaking and applied for teaching positions, although school was in the second quarter. Roy began his new position at the Pentagon. Commuting to and from Washington D.C. and the suburbs was a three-hour chunk of his day. His alarm went off at 4:30 a.m. and he crashed into bed between 8:30 and 9 p.m. After exploring several transportation choices, he had found the simplest way to get to and from work was to join a "Slug Line."

For those of you who have not experienced this urban/suburban phenomenon, allow me to inform. Washington D.C.- bound workers living in the surrounding suburbs line up at a large shopping center or centralized parking lot in towns such as Stafford, Woodbridge, or Springfield. There, one awaits a ride with a total stranger who benefits by putting two or more people in the car to take the High Occupancy Vehicle (HOV) lane into the nation's capital.

Said stranger might be a mild-mannered "pencil-pusher," an elegant career woman with a garbage bag of dirty diapers in the back seat, or a possibly psychopathic husband swilling a beer and brandishing a handgun toward his nagging wife. These are not embellished characterizations. Roy's most dramatic accounts of his "slugging" to and from work gave me the horrors. This Miami girl learned young: you NEVER got into a car with an unfamiliar face unless you were incredibly stupid or "high."

I wondered if the daily commute kept Roy on-edge or angry. At the time, I attributed his tension to the demands of his new position in the hallowed halls of the U.S. military's central hub. Paperwork poured in from his superiors, demanding accountability for supplies scattered like pick-up sticks from Florida City to the Gulf of Mexico. After-action reports of salvage efforts and certifications had to be generated, even as he was adjusting to more demands in his new position, working in a tiny cubicle with a smattering of light gleaming off a concrete wall. In the "Puzzle Palace," where more than 20,000 military and civilians worked, his head spun, as a bustling crowd practically shoved him to the right side of the Metro system escalators. Once, when I went with him into D.C. for the day, I saw women in blazers and skirts, silk scarves flying behind their necks, zooming around us in Adidas and Reebok high-tops, their three-inch stilettos in their backpack or large handbag. In the daily blur, I could see why my husband had no time to sort out his emotions.

He had tried and given up taking a commuter train from Woodbridge into Washington for two reasons: It was pricey; and then, there was that one night.

Remember, this was the pre-flip phone era. He was running very late, and the kids had eaten dinner. My imagination played out several drastic scenarios. Was he locked down in an emergency inside the Pentagon and couldn't call me? Had there been a train or car wreck?

Much to my relief, he called me from a payphone in Stafford, the last southbound stop on the line, and asked me to come and get him.

"What on earth?" I thought, and sighed. This meant a fifty- minute round trip before he would have a late dinner. Exhausted, he'd fallen asleep on the train and missed his stop. His car was in the now-closed parking garage at the train station in Woodbridge. From then on, he was "slugging," quickly memorizing the cars with sketchy characters at the wheel.

The Washington pace was like no other in his career. One night, before his early collapse into bed, I broke through his cycle of silent, then growly angst, urging him to tell me if anything specific was dragging him down.

"I just feel sad all the time," he said.

Roy had been keeping his feelings inside. I, on the other hand, was unleashing emotion with writing. Long after everyone had gone to sleep, I sat in the quiet basement, night after night, pounding away on the new computer keyboard. Surrounded by dark, with the low hum of electrical current and heated air moving through the ductwork, I sat in a small circle of lamplight, startling occasionally to unfamiliar pops and knocks of a two-story house. Refocusing on calm and unpacking memories, I stayed up late, processing loss and hard-learned lessons, expounding on journal entries, and reviving my old love of writing poetry.

In *Writing Down the Bones,* author Natalie Goldberg inspired me with the guidance: "First thoughts have tremendous energy."[1] Through the rush of cathartic tears, I birthed hundreds of new thoughts. Meanwhile, my tired husband was consumed by the flood of work at the Pentagon: balancing Air Force policy with random phone calls from survivors from his old crew at Homestead. He had no down-time to consider the ordeal, only a few months behind us. As the worst was over, I wondered, why wasn't he feeling better?

Perhaps it was "pillow talk" many nights later, but we began to speak our feelings of loss. "It wasn't just losing a home and school and leaving Mom and Dad," I told him. "A whole community died that night. Not literally, of course, but one day we were all there together, making our plans for the next Supply party, the promised trip to the Bahamas for the kids . . . then we all blew away. No farewells, no "roasts" and parting gag-gifts, no change of command with the next Supply boss. Full stop. Everyone gone."

In the dim light filtering into our room from the street, he nodded, then sighed. Another deeper exhale. I rolled from my back and laid an arm across his chest.

"That's it," he said, brushing at the corner of his eyes with thumb and forefinger, then settling his arm over mine.

The "family" made up of the hard-workers and the slackers, alike; the Desert Storm veterans and the fresh-faced airmen assigned to their first duty station, all his 31st Supply squadron at Homestead had disappeared. One day, a team of co-workers; the next, a void. Two-hundred-twenty individuals, "his people," scattered all over the globe after that historic night. The loss of their camaraderie hit like sudden accidental death. His grief had been bleeding out in irritability. The abrupt turn in our lives left him longing for closure that would never come. We never said "goodbye."

"Isn't it strange," I murmured in the near-dark, "that despite an almost-new home with almost all new stuff, seeing the kids getting involved in school, making new friends, and loving our new church, we don't feel totally relieved?"

I lay quiet, waiting. He didn't answer. The rhythm of his breathing whispered for him: fast asleep.

For so many late nights, with the moon waxing and waning in the starry space over Washington and Tampa and Homestead, I tiptoed into deeper prayer, pausing as I wrote, to approach the One I called My Heavenly Father.

"Why, God, have you brought us to and through catastrophe?"

How many times had I heard my earthly father recite his King James version of Romans 8:28: "And we know that all things work together for good to them that love God, to them who are the called according to his purpose?"

As a teacher, I have often viewed life as a series of events with lessons. And I was now a student with so many questions: How does this grief work to our "good?" If we loved God, was that enough? Was that what it meant to be "the called?" What were we supposed to learn?

Could it be that He, the One who saved us in the storm, had put us through the crucible of suffering helplessness against the brunt of the hurricane to refine us, to steel our faith? And would a day come when we would offer praise not only as survivors, but as true believers, standing as witnesses that "all things work together to our good," even as we crawl to our feet in the wreckage and the rubble, feeling small and brief as a spark?

So much to sort through. The cardboard boxes around me in the dim recesses of the basement sat in quiet reproach. We still clung to familiar and damaged things. Our tight hands had not yet learned the relief of uncurling from things which never truly satisfy our deepest hunger. But Roy and I had at last realized the flashes of anger and the sorrow cloaked around our shoulders were ghosts of our grief. We recognized a brief life in Homestead and Miami was dead. All things *would* work to our good. Living with that needed time.

Schooled

Gladly would he learn, and gladly teach.

~ Geoffrey Chaucer

Woodbridge 1992-1993

Weird. By summer's end in '92, I was anticipating the new school year, but now, after our mid-fall arrival, I was not following busses into a faculty parking lot. Instead, I kissed Jimmy goodbye at the bus stop and watched new driver Seana ease out of the driveway with Kris. It felt odd, as though I was playing "hooky."

Teacher pre-planning was supposed to start the Monday the hurricane roared out of town. I taught seventh grade Language Arts and Upper School Yearbook at a small private school in Miami. Although the school's theatre teacher was firmly entrenched, I had all the drama I wanted laying out pages of the school's annual and playing referee to young editors with conflicting artistic differences. Only a few days before evacuating, I had completed the seventh grade's summer reading list, including *The Red Pony* and *Where the Red Fern Grows*. I was disappointed I never got to study them with my students. How I loved sharing literature with young people, who always taught me a fresh perspective!

The timing of the move meant my only option for working in the school system was as a substitute teacher. Prince William County offered me a position for the Spring term. During the interview, I told the supervisor I was open to short or long-term jobs. Subbing, by its very nature, is difficult. From the students' point of view, a substitute teacher is a *persona non grata.* Remember your classrooms under the wary eye of the substitute? Mayhem? Undercover vices? Full-on disaster? My own full-time students would learn early each year: "disrespect a sub teacher, you are "dissing" me. I taught with a sense of humor, but never smiled during these instructions. A good substitute teacher's worth is never equal to the subsequent paycheck.

I believe the county office wanted to test my commitment. First assignment: three days in Special Ed, an autism classroom at a middle school. I remember thinking, "How difficult could this be? Class sizes are smaller, more one-on-one . . ." I had taught special students mainstreamed into my classes, but never taken the helm in a special needs classroom.

Then I found out why the teacher was absent. Just married, she had changed her last name. One of her students surprised her with a chair for a wedding gift. He hurled it against her head. In the assistant teacher's opinion, the name-change had triggered his attack. She was in the hospital, expected to recover, and the student had another day of suspension, before he would return.

I was on my guard immediately. The boy *would return* before I left. There were only about six to seven students in the room. I had an assistant and student aide, and found I was not expected to lead activities, but to be part of the team. What a relief! We worked on handouts in reading, geography, and math, and I became a student again of my own profession. Patience and cheers for small positive steps were the key.

At that point in my career, I had known few special ed teachers, as we tended to flock by department. I hadn't a clue that working with an autistic preteen girl meant teaching her not to bring a soiled sanitary pad out of the bathroom for all to see, and to remind her to pull her panties up. I learned that many of the students' little squalls passed quickly; shouting and tears came and went in a volatile brew of early adolescence and their special needs.

At the end of the first day, I sat trembling on the edge of our bed, scrawling a few thoughts into my journal. Roy and I had three healthy children. At this point, they tackled age-appropriate life tasks and handled their homework without assistance. Their behavior was socially appropriate. Humbled, I bowed my head. Other parents were out in the world, working all day, then coming home to children needing their care every waking hour. Why were we given such grace?

Silently, I cried myself to sleep that night and woke to face the second day. I braced myself. No way would I wimp out. The decision to stay on the job proved providential.

Before class began, one of the student aides chatted with me about my teaching experience. When I told her I hoped to find a drama teaching job again, she perked up.

"My brother goes to high school in Manassas, and they've had a sub in drama for, like, over a couple of months. The teacher had some health issues. Nobody knows if she will be back. I think they have to get a new sub soon, because the one there now can't stay."

I made a mental note: find Manassas.

The remainder of my temporary stay in the autism class went without incident. The child who injured his teacher never threatened me. I still returned home at the end of the day, amazed that my own parenting role was so easy, and knowing that I would never again take my children's physical or mental health for granted.

§§§

Approaching the receptionist in the main office of a school might be compared to approaching the main gate of a military base. You had better know exactly why you want access beyond the "welcome desk," and qualifications are helpful. With a resumé in hand, when I stated the purpose of my visit and mentioned previous teaching experience, the smiling receptionist introduced me to Assistant Principal Howell. He was delighted that I'd heard about the drama position. During the impromptu interview, he inquired about my first Virginia high school experience as a theatre director during our Langley Air Force Base years; then, smiling, he immediately dialed up a colleague in the county office.

How could this be? Hundreds of administrators from one end of the state to another and suddenly I am on Mr. Howell's speakerphone, chatting with one of my former assistant principals, about my family's two years in Turkey and our "up-close-and-personal" encounter with Andrew. She gave her endorsement on the spot, and cheery Mr. Howell welcomed me with instructions to show up the next day to observe two English and four drama classes. He advised me to be prepared to take them over the following week.

After my observation day, my cheeks sore from smiling all day at the curious young faces stealing looks, while their sub worked her way through her last day, I prayed for a way to reach them. I needed them to know I understood the stress of having a sick drama director, with multiple subs assigning work, but without degrees in the subject. I had lived through a long Miami teacher strike in the ninth grade. How we longed for our regular instructors and resented "subs" entering six-week grades on our report cards! Adding to their misery, these students had been forced to cancel their spring play.

During the night, came a whisper. "Look down." *Down* was the key word . . . right downstairs to the boxes in the basement. We had begun sorting through items which at first look, were not damaged enough to toss out, and those beginning to look hopelessly water stained. So many salvaged cookbooks, videotapes, compact discs, and framed photos to examine. One of my dearest baby photos of Jim was doomed. Darkly bubbled and rippled in the corners of the frame, the photo adhered to the tar-speckled glass. It was the perfect metaphor.

In English Lit and Theatre classes, I pulled the small frame out of my purse after I'd re-introduced myself and called the roll. I told the students I wanted to show them something. Curiosity is a strong educational tool. Up and down the aisles between the desks, I walked, asking, "What do you think happened here?" Of course, I got questions.

"Is that your baby?"

"How old is he?"

Many of the students guessed the picture had been through a fire. Briefly, I told them about Andrew's impact on my family. Some had heard of the storm less than a year before and uttered sympathies.

"We've all been through storms," I said. "Yours has taken place over the past few months. I know some of you are hurting. But this ten-year old picture of my son reminds me that even in pain, we accept our losses, pick up, and move on. We're going to move through what's left of this year together."

God had answered my prayer.

After a few days, I knew I had a cooperative and eager

group of teens, pleased to have an experienced drama teacher. And if students accepted my directorial discretion over choice of script, a spring play was still possible. An excited buzz followed: the "sub" was willing to mount a production without being hired for a full-time position.

It was an easy decision. I truly loved theatre, the students were motivated and supportive of me, and I didn't need a financial supplement for motivation. I chose a classic classroom comedy/drama I knew well: *Up the Down Staircase*. Not only had I directed it in southern Virginia, but I'd also performed the play in both Miami and Hawaii. At Kailua High, a month before graduation, I played the leading role: a high school teacher. Prophetic, indeed.

My department head approved of my work as a Literature and Theatre Arts sub and invited me to apply for a fellowship with the Northern Virginia Writing Project, a part of the National Writing Project, encouraging teachers to get students writing across the curriculum. I leapt at the opportunity.

Twenty plus educators from schools all over Northern Virginia met at George Mason University the following summer. Surrounded by a group of colleagues who loved teaching as much as I did, I workshopped my first revision of scraps and scribblings from my journal into three chapters about my encounter with Andrew. These formed the foundation of this story. And in the middle of that summer, while attending the program, my subbing days in Manassas slipped into history. I signed a contract for a full-time position for the 1993-94 school year.

In a quavering voice that summer, for the first time, I began to publicly acknowledge awareness of God's Spirit moving through my life. Like stone laid on stone, one event led to another, cementing my belief that nothing, not one event in my life, was random.

Roads Back to Grit and Ghosts

Be gracious to me, O Lord, for I am languishing; heal me,
O Lord, for my bones are troubled.

~ Psalm 6:2

Woodbridge,   **1992-1993**

Watching Northern Virginia's seasons change reminded
us that we, too, were changing. Japanese maples in our
neighborhood had burst aflame with color, followed by the
wondrous silence of a cloak of fresh snow. We longed for
the lightness of the coming spring after bearing the weight
of a wearisome year.

How often has a seed of optimism promised to bloom as
we look back on the course of healing after a broken bone,
a broken heart, or a broken place? With a relieved sigh, we
admit, "Okay. I am feeling a bit better. . .that's over with."
Yet, sometimes, we slip back on the rocks and gravel of
a long climb toward the green of restoration. It hurts. A
few more tears fall. For some of us, balance returns. Deep
breaths. We seek a foothold once again. When we want to
live, we hold fast to flowering hope.

We thought we were gaining firm footing, restarting a
new normal, far from South Florida. While each of us was
breaking-in a new routine at school or work, the Air Force
arrived one Saturday morning. No, not the entire Air Force,

157

but a military-contracted moving van. Gears grinding, a semi-tractor trailer hissed to a stop alongside our curb.

As its driver and co-pilot rattled open the sliding doors, we recognized the sorry, soggy furnishings we'd tried to leave behind. Our bedroom furniture, seams still swollen, were mere warped wooden boxes, their hidden treasure forever locked inside. Seconds later, the post-storm stench exuded from the van and engulfed us. Uncanny, how our sense of smell drags us back into places we've fled before.

"Take it away! Keep it or dump it somewhere if you have to!" Roy begged the driver. We never expected to again see what we'd left behind. All had been replaced.

The nonplussed driver had his delivery instructions. For a couple of minutes, we had to convince him, we neither had space for nor interest in more salvage from Homestead. It felt like a grave had been reopened. A swell of nausea swept over me.

"Please take it," I pleaded. "We'll sign that you attempted to deliver, and we refused. Please drop it off at a Salvation Army or Goodwill store. Someone can use a good washer and dryer." They had been sealed in a room without damage.

Before the reluctant trucker pulled away, we had accepted the return of our formal dining room furniture, our kitchen table set, and several boxes labeled "LtCol. Jardin/Kitchen." Unwrapping dirty casserole dishes, flatware, and everyday dishes, we raced to load the dishwasher to keep the stink of stormwater from permeating our new home.

Down to the basement went our old dining room suite until our friends, the Scotts, arrived to check out our new house and take the set home to Smithfield for restoration. The rattan and glass kitchen set was salvageable and one of our dearest Italian souvenirs, purchased just before our little "dual-national," Jimmy, was born in Vicenza. The glass top proved durable through ocean transport and tempest, but tar-paper flecks infected all its nooks and crannies.

For several days on the outside deck, battling flashbacks of our ruined home, I donned garden gloves and wielded a stiff-bristled brush to remove slivers of glass caught in the wicker wrapping around every chair and table leg. S-c-ritch – s-c-ritch, fierce and relentless, I swiped, then wiped with a towel soaked with WD-40®. Determined, I *would* remove all the traces of Andrew's fury. He would not hurl the last punch in our fight to put him down, once and for all. The storm was dead, and we were coming back to life.

In her inspirational work, *Placemaker,* about "tending, keeping and caring" for the places we call home, author Christie Purifoy writes, "Loss is painful, sometimes catastrophic, but like some terrible, black soil it also has the potential to bear exquisite fruit." [1]We were still in the dark dirt and grit of our losses, but hopeful. Much later, as is the case of most trials of life, we would taste of that "exquisite fruit." But not yet.

As though in mourning, the table and chair legs wept tar streaks for months after my thorough cleaning. Black, pencil-thin trails appeared on our tile floor, as we pulled into and pushed away from our "daily bread." I began to wonder if God intended to keep our healing slow. Each piercing arrow of memory pointed us back to Him, the One who gives and takes away. On its own schedule, a wound heals in the body. And so it is with the hurting soul.

Yet, it wasn't about the stuff left inside our walls, it was about the stuff inside ourselves. Seana, Krissie, and Jimmy couldn't yet see the lessons they had already learned in a few short months. They had attended their Riverview schools for weeks, where they had no friends, while working through the sadness of their own sudden personal losses. So many familiar old playthings, books, and travel memorabilia gone. They had accepted the charity of strangers–friends of their Aunt Carol and Uncle Ralph–arriving at the door, acting as the "hands and feet of Jesus," offering clothing and toys for each of them. In Woodbridge, as they enrolled in school for the second time in the fall semester, already chapters behind, they jumped into new subjects and flourished. Embedded now in their lives was a new facet of education: grace under pressure, supplemented by firm spiritual leadership from our youth pastors at All Saints Church.

In our own healing journey, it hadn't yet occurred to me to pray with my husband, as we do now. I never even asked Roy if he was praying. But I was. While he slogged and slugged his way into the heart of the nation's capital each day, I was gifted twice a day with twenty-five minutes of quiet travel time. It was my first year of school travel without the children aboard, and my first regular encounter with a daily period of solitude.

With the radio turned off, I headed west to Manassas, spared the madness of Washington-bound traffic. On the way to work, I found myself spending that time reaching out to God. Aloneness after the season of storm permitted me to ponder my recent past and to begin a period of repentance. It was a gift of time, but not always comfortable.

Henri Nouwen, in *The Way of the Heart,* describes solitude in practical, searching terms: "In solitude I get rid of my scaffolding: no friends to talk with no telephone calls to make, no meetings to attend, no music to entertain, no books to distract, just me-naked, vulnerable, weak, sinful, deprived, broken-nothing. It is this nothingness that I have to face in my solitude, a nothingness so dreadful that everything in me wants to run to my friends, my work, and my distractions so that I can forget my nothingness and make myself believe that I am worth something. But that is not all. As soon as I decide to stay in my solitude, confusing ideas, disturbing images, wild fantasies, and weird associations jump about in my mind like monkeys in a banana tree...."[2]

"Disturbing images," more like wraiths than monkeys, swirled into my solitary reflection. For two years in Turkey, I had acted out in uncharacteristic rebellion before arriving at Homestead. Was it a "mid-life crisis"? I couldn't say. All I knew was while I had buried it for a couple of busy years, the time had come to stare it down. I had to admit I'd made some poor choices during a season when the terrain of our marriage was shaky and uncertain.

§§§

Marital tremors had begun in earnest in 1987, while Roy was stationed at Langley Air Force Base in southern Virginia. He brought home orders to serve in the Joint Military Mission for Aid to Turkey, officially acronymed "JUSMMAT," the best of the alternatives, which had included Saudi Arabia, Guam, or Woomera, Australia. At a crossroads between Western and Eastern cultures, Turkey's capital city, Ankara, was a gathering place for diplomats from all over the world. It sounded exciting and exotic. Plus, it was only a two-year assignment. I thought I had known what to expect when we embarked on my husband's military career. I would go where he went. Yet, my husband almost journeyed alone to that crossroads. Preparation for our entire family was complex and emotionally charged.

From October through April, before our transfer, Roy made only three brief stops at home and then was gone again. In a series of temporary duties (TDY's) from Illinois to California to Florida, he attended courses in foreign military sales, Turkish language, and anti-terrorism training. This came on the heels of two years spent mostly apart in South Carolina, as he traveled with an inspection team out of Shaw Air Force Base. At least there, in nearby Columbia, Roy's parents and brother, Craig, and his wife, Betty, had offered family support through minor crises.

The seventies birthed the term "Super-Mom." It was still a thriving concept in the late eighties. A mother's assignment: raise kids, run the household like a CEO, and be outstanding in a full-time (successful) career. Oh, wait! There was more. Media set the standard for the "modern woman": Perm your hair, no matter how clownish you look (straight hair and unpadded shoulders were so "yesterday"); dazzle him with your *Dirty Dancing* moves; be cool and a tad tough with your *Top Gun*; and try not to be as clueless as the mom in *Ferris Bueller's Day Off*. So much to achieve.

The descriptor "stressed-out" was also born in the same era. It became my mantra. Our children were in preschool through middle school; I was teaching full-time high school drama to help pay the double debt of rent and the mortgage for our unsold South Carolina home. While acting as ringmaster and acrobat in the center ring of a circus, juggling parenting as both mom and dad, I teetered along a tightrope of sanity. Snippets of time spent with my re-found friend Diane Scott often helped me cope, but she was a full-time high school teacher as well, living in Smithfield, over the river and through a snaggle of downtown Newport News traffic. She and Richard were also tangled in medical testing of their little Jennifer, who had begun exhibiting symptoms of a rare metabolic disease. Neither of us had anything resembling spare time.

In this lonely reality, for the first time during Roy's extended absences, how my heart went out to parents who assume a working single-parent role without a choice! My minor "pot-holes" loomed large: getting my first speeding ticket as I rushed home after rehearsal, running late in picking up the kids; losing pizza dinner money in the winter-dark Food Lion parking lot, as I wrangled three tired, hungry, small people and a cart of groceries; and crying occasionally on the way to school, listening to Richard Marx singing, "Right Here Waiting," with lyrics perfectly capturing the pain of our separation. We had no Facetime or Zoom calls in the "old days." Long-distance calls added to bills we were already struggling to pay.

We were waiting for Roy, all right, but when he came home for a couple of weeks of holiday leave, he found the festive house full of visiting relatives, an exhausted wife, and three amped-up kids who couldn't get enough iced gingerbread or his attention.

Christmas was rushed and strained, hardly offering the cozy closeness of the crackling fire we'd imagined. As two young working parents, finding time and inclination for intimacy had been a bad joke for a while. Somewhere deep down, when I could bear peering into the dark corners of our twelve-year old marriage, I had to admit that absence failed to make the heart grow fonder. Perhaps sensing this in long-distance pep-talks, my world-wise and generous Dad offered a belated Christmas gift: a round trip ticket for winter break weekend to Monterey, California, the site of Roy's language school. As a bonus, he and Libby would fly up from Miami to babysit (spoil) their grandkids for a few days.

Although it had the trappings of a second honeymoon, the two of us exploring living postcards of breezy Carmel, Pebble Beach, and San Francisco's Fisherman's Wharf, our time together was tinged with unspoken tension. One evening, as we curved back and forth in his rental car, hugging the serpentine Pacific Coast along the Big Sur Highway, my husband chattered about Defense Language Institute, even teaching me to recite a few numbers in Turkish. With years of Spanish behind me and a smattering of French, I fretted about communicating in a foreign country with an Arabic-based language. How would I navigate the city of Ankara without comprehension? He changed the subject and told stories of cracking jokes with classmates; like errant adolescents, they'd pranked a substitute instructor by placing all their chairs on the desks during a break and skipping the end of a class.

He described some of his peers who came from all branches of the military. I was troubled that one of his newfound buddies was an enthusiastic fan of the "Open Marriage" philosophy, popularized in the seventies. Wise choice of friends? I wondered. I had read the book and could not understand why married people would give one another permission for intimacy with other partners, after agreeing on their "terms." Roy and I married committed to monogamy, sharing our vows to "forsake all others. . . for better or worse. . .'til death do us part." What kind of assurance came with open marriage; and what kind of fellowship did one have with a man who touted mutual sexual freedom for married partners?

With more separations coming, I flew home unsettled. The old military adage, "What happens TDY, stays TDY," often exchanged between buddies with a wink-wink and a jovial elbow bump, not only left me cold; it made me anxious and suspicious. Trusting people who loved me had never come easily.

Our brief "honeymooner's weekend" over, I hadn't been home long when one of Roy's co-workers called. It was late and I had just put the kids to bed. I scarcely knew the man on the other end of the line.

"Hi! I know Roy's been gone for a while. How are you doing?"

After the exchange of pleasantries: "Nice of you to call . . . (awkward silence) The kids and I are hanging in there…" (another uneasy pause). I was eager to sit down and get to work designing some lesson plans.

"Say," he continued, "How about going out to dinner one night?

"Oh, that's very nice of you to offer, but I don't think so."

He pressed on. "Come on, it's not a date. I just would like to treat you to a meal, maybe get a sitter and have a relaxed evening out?"

Dinner for two. In the absence of my spouse. I knew enough to suspect where this offer might be coming from, and I did my best to be polite. "Probably not but thank you."

He persisted. "I'm talking just dinner – you know. I'd really like to get you out of the house for an evening."

How thoughtful of him to sense my loneliness! How odd and out of character would it be to accept this invitation? And, by the way, I thought, why the insistence? What was his marital status? Was he another "Open Marriage" enthusiast?

As soon as I was able, I ended the call, thanking him once more for thinking of me in Roy's extended TDY. Perhaps I should have been grateful he cared enough to call. Maybe he was guileless? Whatever his true agenda, I was not going out with any man—especially one I really didn't know outside my husband's office.

Plunged back into a crush of distrust, I seethed. Was this a military-lifestyle thing? "Loosey-goosey" marriage arrangements and dates-not-really dates? I mulled over the discomfort of our separation. Was I so naïve to believe that once married, most couples guarded their relationship from temptation to cheat? My imagination was working overtime, and I couldn't wait until our family was intact again.

Together again by Easter, we scrubbed up pretty for the annual spring photos. I've since looked at the pictures of the children's sweet faces, shining with relief that Daddy was home. Didn't we look like an almost perfect American family? The caption might have read, "Two escapees of the hippie-free-love era and the drug-mad disco seventies. Still happily married with children." Well, we were still married. With children. No one would have guessed what was going on behind the snapshots.

Groans Too Deep for Words

The course of true love never did run smooth.

~Shakespeare, *A Midsummer Night's Dream*

Poquoson, 1988

Roy was home, proficient in Turkish language and anti-terrorist tactics; I had graduated from his string of TDY's with an advanced degree in self-sufficiency. The children and I had to work him back onto the home team. Alone, among other issues, I had managed the broken furnace on a fourteen-degree school morning, a passive-aggressive revolt from a few drama kids about the "unfair" casting of the spring musical, and backchat from our two pre-teens facing another uprooting. Single parents do it all the time, I realized. That was the problem. Reluctantly, I had grown accustomed to being a "single mom."

We were in trouble. Battle-weary, I was relieved Roy was back, but had little left to give my husband. He was tanned and re-energized from what was practically vacation, with a touch of "class," sporting cozy photos of wining and dining on the West Coast with newfound friends, male and female. He was hungry for time with me. I was starving for rest and time alone. Fully alone. I needed a TDY—possibly to Antarctica–with or without wine- a place where no one needed me for anything.

Our conflicts erupted behind closed doors. When we fought, it was almost always about how to raise our children or how to spend money. I believed he was too hard and demanding as a parent; he thought I was too soft and lenient. He wanted to buy new stereo equipment; I wanted to save for our upcoming move. Roy was never afraid to wrangle an issue, even if it meant loud resolution. Having observed so much conflict in my youth, I loathed a fight and avoided confrontation whenever possible. Each of us still wrestled with heart-to-heart communication, and we settled for "small talk" or worse, silence, to keep the peace.

We'd become opposing rockets, our trajectories taking us toward opposite ends of outer space. For the first time in our lives, I wondered if we really loved one another anymore, or if I was just making life easier for him to pursue his career. I asked him to go to marriage counseling, and he agreed.

Our counselor, Amanda, booked us for several counseling sessions, individually and together. When we went as a couple, we sat side-by-side, but not touching, on her dark leather couch. We read homework hand-outs about keeping married love alive without the expectation of maintaining all the dreamy, breathless romance of a honeymoon. She prodded us to confront the illusion that a wedding ceremony buries all the burdens we carry from our youth. At last, we voiced feelings we had tried to keep from each other: doubts about our compatibility, feelings of being unloved or unappreciated, missing the sparkle of our early attraction to one another. Buried, unspoken wounds surfaced. Tears and apologies co-mingled. Progress.

We still had to learn that forgiveness for past hurts was a process. But our time before the move to Ankara was short. Forced to end the sessions before we were ready, we thanked Amanda for her guidance and told her we were not planning a divorce. Her face reflected delight and relief.

"That isn't always the way it goes in my business," she said.

"Keep talking," was her adieu.

But, late into the nights, I stared at the streetlight filtering through the blinds, thinking about staying in the States with the children, keeping them in their schools, myself in my job, and letting Roy go on to Turkey alone. After all, there was danger; occasional random acts of terror were still being committed by radical extremists. Maybe extended time apart would test the strength of our bond. But I had always dreaded the separation of a one-year "remote assignment," required of most military members, and we had barely survived the six-month preparatory time for our next assignment. At least this tour would keep our family together, while giving Roy credit for the "remote" year. There was *that*.

The school year ended. My drama students held their year-end banquet. Some of them were still convinced I hadn't fully appreciated their talents. Only two of my most dedicated and loyal thespians gave me a parting gift. Period. It felt as though the others had said, "See ya, Mrs. J. Have a nice trip and don't let the door hit you as you exit Stage Left."

Professionally and personally, I felt I had failed. If life was to be savored, it had a bitter aftertaste, reinforcing old and new insecurities, fears that I was not only a mediocre wife, but also a forgettable teacher.

At home, I sank into dark doubt and self-loathing. It would be years before I had enough confidence in myself as an educator, that my students' respect was a far bigger prize than their fandom. I wasn't sure I had the capacity to be a good enough spouse for Roy. Had I devoted all my energy to loving my children at the cost of not cherishing my husband? After all, we'd promised to love one another before we became parents.

Through this unhappy season, I had a "Sunday-go-to-church" connection with God and no regular prayer life. He was essentially like a genie in a bottle. If I pressed my palms together just right as I prayed, perhaps He would answer. I wasn't wise enough, then, to dig into the Bible for help, and had no spiritual guidance. We attended Mass regularly at the chapel on base, but with no other contact with our priest. Long before, I had accepted Jesus the Messiah's life, death, and resurrection was to save sinners like me. If God really sees it all, and I'm worth saving, I thought, maybe He'd give me just a little hint of what I should do?

Looking back at those days in my rear-view mirror, despite my lack of faith and fear for the future, I believe I was divinely steered toward keeping our nest together. Even those years while I was not growing in my relationship with my Creator, He was there in the day-to-day. One day, I would understand how prayers are answered, even when we don't know how to pray.

In his letter to the Romans, St. Paul writes: *"Likewise the Spirit helps us in our weakness. For we do not know what to pray for as we ought, but the Spirit himself intercedes for us with groanings too deep for words.[1]*

Whatever my struggle, I was soon going to realize that God already knew my story. If Roy and I needed to strengthen our marriage, it couldn't happen half-a-world apart for two years. The prospect of a hiatus from the "Super-Mom" role had appeal.

The next challenge following Roy's separation from us was making the "Permanent-Change-of-Station" preparations. In Ankara, the British Embassy would provide our furnished four-bedroom apartment in the diplomatic district, so we organized our household into four-pronged preparation. As aforementioned, only 2,000 pounds would be allowed for shipment overseas—quite the limit when a one-bedroom home is estimated to weigh in at 3,000 pounds.

In one corner of the rental house was a small collection known as "hold baggage," temporary living items: an assortment of kitchen/bedroom/bathroom essentials, minimal wardrobe, and personal grooming supplies. Then, the balance of small kitchen appliances, dishes and glassware, electronics, favorite films, music and books, blankets and bedding, and a four-season sampler of our attire was collected in another room. In another corner was the contents of our suitcases. Everything else in the house was packed for long-term storage. We promised the children that when the two-year tour of Turkey was finished, receiving our tons of old familiar things would feel like Christmas.

In June 1988, at Langley Air Force Base, we posed for our Diplomatic Passport photos and attended farewell parties. I was still fraught with doubts about the move. I agonized about learning to speak Turkish with the locals. *¿Se habla Español?* was not going to offer the slightest sliver of help. But more than that, with the abrupt end to our marital counseling, Roy and I had our own communication to work on. We had the tickets and an itinerary, but I still had reservations about the tour.

On My Knees, Behind the Wheel

You can't go back and change the beginning, but you can start where you are and change the ending.

~ C.S. Lewis

Ankara 1988-1990

Once there, I was glad I agreed to go along on our Turkish adventure. The Turks were cordial and hospitable. Their cuisine, Mid-Eastern, but influenced by the French, was superb, especially the *eskinder*: shaved roasted lamb with the flavor and tenderness of veal. The aroma of the lamb hanging on a giant vertical spit in a local restaurant, mingling with burnt coal and diesel fuel wafted through downtown Ankara, bustling with people of global nationalities. In shops and kiosks, merchants offered hot glasses of chai tea or warm yoghurt-based *ayran*, while we shopped.

Artifacts from thousands of years of history lay before us, all over the country. Travel and accommodations were inexpensive by American standards. Alongside the crystalline sapphire Aegean Sea, we vacationed at Didim, site of remains of an ancient temple of Apollo. Without a box of cereal in sight, the children tasted their first truly local breakfast of cucumbers, tomatoes, olives, and eggs. Everyone's favorite was the hot, buttered *ekmek*—the Turk's delicious bread. We scrabbled over ruins and stood in amazement in the Grand Theatre in Ephesus where the Apostle Paul had incited a riot. We skied the Bursa

Mountains and clambered through the hive-like caves of Cappadocia, hiding place to early persecuted Christians. We hoped those two years of family adventures would make memories the children would carry into their adulthood.

Despite the travel and sightseeing opportunities, many Americans overseas sorely miss the comforts of the U.S.A.—their favorite television shows and Friday night movies without subtitles, drive-through meals, and shopping in air-conditioned malls. So they seek diversions they would probably avoid back in the States. That's when I began ironing out some of my insecurities in an uncharacteristic fashion.

Along with others in the JUSMMAT crowd, Roy and I began regularly going to the Officer's Club on Friday nights for drinking and dancing. We would leave after the children's bedtime, as Seana was old enough to babysit her brother and sister. Other adults, including the landlord, or *kapaçi*, were scattered around our apartment building, so we knew she could find help if needed. But I look back in horror–especially at an era without cell phones–and can't believe I was so lackadaisical, so sure that our children would be safe until midnight in a downtown Ankara apartment.

Had there been calamity, I would have blamed myself forever. Many years later, when it was safe to confess some of their youthful sins to us, the three children admitted they'd delighted in decadent cahoots, having unchaperoned Friday night fun of their own. They'd invented a game of repeated leaping and cavorting from pieces of furniture scattered around the living room. Thank God none of them ever knocked out a tooth or broke any bones. (If there was any other chicanery, they're taking it to their graves.)

Going to the club, for me, was not about the bar.

Remember, I'd started my freshman year at Baylor University as a "rule-following goody-two-shoes girl." I had been the most ardent teetotaler through my college years. I didn't even like wine when we married. Once I was of legal drinking age, my father sometimes mixed for me a Coke with just a splash of rum, when he served drinks at home. But hard liquor had no appeal. Despite all the accompanying foods everyone recommended with beer: pizza, picnic fare, subs at the beach, I had no interest in brew either. Mostly, I had avoided alcohol because so many of my peers drank themselves sick. I couldn't imagine anything less fun than "tossing my cookies" (and drinks) in the front seat of someone's car.

I joined the regular Friday night crowd because I loved to dance. Roy, with natural rhythm as a drummer, claimed he "couldn't" dance, but was content to rock me gently back and forth in his arms to the slow songs. And he didn't seem to mind co-workers asking me to dance. Sometimes he let himself be dragged to dance floor with someone else's wife; but usually he sat at a table for five or six, chatting amiably. He preferred telling jokes and talking shop, to disco dancing. I wasn't going to sit, waiting for him.

Several months into our tour, with the services of a Turkish housekeeper who worked for American military families, one after another, as they rotated through their two-year stints, I found myself hungry to do something besides shop and sightsee. After a few weeks of substitute teaching at the American base school, followed by a brief opportunity to write company policies for a U.S. contractor, I passed a minimal typing test and secured a government secretarial position in JUSMMAT Headquarters, where Roy worked. It was the first time as a couple we could discuss sensitive information about threats affecting Americans abroad. Also, a first: high-ranking officers from Army and Air Force hovering over my shoulders as I pounded out urgent messages on the office computer to concerned government agencies. Releasing job-related tension, I enjoyed socializing at week's end with fellow workers. Some of these newfound friends at the club took turns buying rounds of drinks. They encouraged me to try something more exotic than a splash of rum in Coke. Suddenly at thirty-five, I thought, "Why not? Have I missed something?"

For the first time in my life, men, married or not, were flattering and flirting with me. This was a peculiar turnabout. Throughout our courtship and even into our marriage, I had endured other girls and women flitting around Roy like little bugs to a porch light. As they giggled over his punch lines, I was not blind to their gazing and body language. With hands flipping their hair or taking playful jabs at him, as he made them laugh, they suggested to him that *if anything* should happen between us, they were right there for him. My uncertainties about love and trust had made me jealous, obsessed with fear of betrayal. Now here I was, dancing in a danger zone with men who also liked to move to the music. I was flummoxed, thrilled by their attention, and ashamed that I enjoyed it.

So far from home and a firm foundation, every Friday night was a party until midnight. Like the drinks, we mixed and swirled in the crowd. Gabbing with others, we avoided making time for hard conversations about us. Roy and I had fallen in love so young, so inexperienced in the world of navigating magnetism between the sexes, and so afraid to talk about it.

Under the gaze of other men, I realized that attraction begins with the eyes, followed by fantasy and curiosity. But I was a girl who, despite longing for approval and wanting to be liked, had grown up looking both ways before crossing the street, being friendly but not forward, loving, but not lustful. I knew the Ten Commandments and was old enough to realize they were laws easily broken. Weakened by doubts about the durability of our marriage and my skills as a teacher, I had wandered into new uncharted terrain, filled with uneven places and deceptive heights. I came so close to losing firm footing and falling from a precipice. I drank Tequila Sunrises and moved to the music until I was weary. What a cringe-worthy picture: our arms linked, Roy steadying my way up the apartment building stairs at evening's end. Then the headachy Saturday mornings, followed by rote worship at Sunday Mass. As I mouthed the words: "Bless me, Father, for I have sinned," I knew I needed to course-correct.

As a mother, I was short-changing my children. Never had I had so much free time to spend with my them. Now, the eyes of hard-won wisdom see those Friday nights as a missed opportunity for playing board games together, reading favorite books aloud, or watching videotapes of U.S. movies and television programs, recorded by stateside family.

§§§

When I left Turkey, I had a scrapbook rich with vacation photos with friends, pictures of local villagers, Aegean beaches, coves and ancient caves, and our children laughing, petting goats and holding tight to saddles on lumbering camels, the "jalopies" of the animal kingdom. In turn, I shed a skin that never suited me and left it there. . . Sometimes, changing locations is a gift. How fitting that we were returning to South Florida, home of my roots, and even in the turbulence, my shelter.

Then, without pause, after the promised stored household goods arrived and found their places in our base house, I was whirling through two years of Homestead days and nights as a squadron commander's wife, a full-time secretary, then teacher, and mom of kids doing drama and sports; I hadn't made time to ponder the tumult of our overseas life. Then came our head-on collision with Andrew.

In my newfound solitude, driving in the Northern Virginia countryside, I found daily confessional time. In effect, I was on my knees in the driver's seat. But the Father's closeness was almost palpable, His Spirit resting beside me. Despite my wondering whether God had used catastrophe to chasten, and then save us, I thanked Him on my silent ride toward Manassas, for knocking us down into the muck to get us to "look up." He'd given us another chance to get it right.

Not long ago, Roy mentioned to a retired friend of ours, Pastor Bill, that for a while, we thought God sent Hurricane Andrew to punish us for our sins. With his typical wit, he grinned and told my husband, "Well, that would sure be a lot of collateral damage." He made his point through our laughter. Why would thousands of people be punished by a windstorm designated to destroy the home of two lowly souls, such as we? On closer evaluation, we agreed our idea smacked of faulty logic.

Perhaps, the storm wasn't directed toward us, but rather, worked to our good, sharpening our focus on the Lord of the Winds.

In my solitude, I prayed, "Father, I know I am broken. I have wandered from the path you set out for me, that I have always known was right and pleasing to you. In studying your Word, I recognize and confess turning away from You, the lover of my soul. The pursuit of empty pleasure and foolish squandering of the time you have given me has been an act of spiritual adultery. Please forgive me for so much selfishness, pride, and for poor choices. . .But, in allowing my stumbling, you have made me a wiser, more caring wife to my husband and a more nurturing momma to my children. You have given me these true loves of my life. Thank you for saving me with your inexpressible and abundant grace. Help me live in Your Light."

Answers to my surrendering prayers came in a comforting commute, leading me through the sanctuary of quiet woods beside burbling clear streams, making a path past majestic horses, peaceful at pasture. Some might call this kind of experience coming to "a closer Walk with the Lord." For me, it was certainly a closer drive. The mornings and afternoons spent on my knees behind the wheel, along with Scripture study with our church community, assured me that although I would never be perfect, I was redeemed by Jesus's death and resurrection.

"This is the God of the gospel of grace," writes laicized priest and author, Brennan Manning. "A God who, out of love for us, sent the only Son He ever had wrapped in our skin. He learned how to walk, stumbled and fell, cried for His milk, sweated blood in the night, was lashed with a whip and showered with spit, was fixed to a cross and died whispering forgiveness on us all." [1]

Truly, I'd been hearing His forgiving whispers for years. At last, I was learning how to listen, as He prepared me for my next step: finding my voice to give glory to Him.

Answering the Call

Jesus said to her, "I am the resurrection and the life.
Whoever believes in me, though he die, yet shall he live,
and everyone who lives and believes in me shall never die.
Do you believe this?"

~ John 11:25-26

Woodbridge – Mid-Nineties

A ringing phone at 8 a.m. on Sunday morning meant something gone sideways. Our routine was to get up, shower, and down a quick breakfast, usually pastry and coffee. Target goal: get to Sunday School, choir rehearsal, and worship on schedule. No one in our extended family called at that hour. I grabbed the portable phone next to our bed and returned to the bathroom vanity.

"Hello?" I said, pausing to check the temperature of the curling wand in the other hand.

"Mrs. Jardin?" Definitely one of my students. A young male voice — not yet recognizable.

It was the morning after the Junior/Senior prom. That hadn't hit me yet.

The voice was quavering and high pitched. "This is Jas."

I had to go through a short list of "Jasons" out of seven speech and drama classes each day.

"Oh, Mrs. Jardin, Mark's dead."

Curling iron dropping into the sink, I cradled the phone now, both hands holding it close. Sixteen year-old Jas was crying. Disjointed words scattered like beads from a broken string and I was trying to put them together through his sobs.

"He got killed–head-on last night–he just dropped off his date."

Colliding thoughts made my head throb: not Mark...surely, he wouldn't drink...such a gentle, sweet boy I'd known through class and mainstage drama productions of *M*A*S*H* and *Flowers for Algernon*. His driver's license was still new. The kids had all sat through the lecture: *"Don't mess with drugs or alcohol on prom night."*

Jas was almost unintelligible now. "He got killed by a drunk."

Mark would have won my "Most Improved Actor" for the year. Sandy-haired, over six feet tall, he was sometimes a little teen-goofy, but always cheerful and well-liked by fellow thespians. At his wake, standing next to a table full of framed pictures of her son at all stages of his brief life, his mother later told me he was less than a mile from home.

She would forever remember the happiness in his voice when he called from his date's house. But five minutes...then fifteen minutes...and he wasn't home right after his call. She began to knot up, those tight, fierce Mama-knots that tether our children to our hearts. Sirens wailed louder toward her neighborhood. She nearly collapsed under the unthinkable, but out into the dark, she rushed on foot, running to the end of her street. From the corner where it met the main road, she saw flashing blue and red. She knew.

The twenty-something who crossed the center line had a purported prior drunk driving offense. Hearing this, several outraged students living in his community filled in the missing details of his collision with Mark. I heard their laments: "He's been sentenced to community service after he recovers from his injuries …. He broke his nose and his arm."

Mark, on the other hand, driving a large family sedan, was crushed as the front end of his car, steering wheel, and dashboard smashed his lanky frame against the driver seat. He died on impact.

His friend, and fellow drama student, Shara, struggled with having been the last person to see him alive. They had arrived side by side at a red light, the multiple lanes ahead merging to a two-lane road just ahead of them. They grinned, playfully gunning their motors at each other, inching forward. The light turned green, and she gave Mark the hand gesture signaling, "After you." He wasn't speeding as he pulled away with a wave, bound for home. Moments later, she saw the smoky burst of the crash ahead and was first on the scene. She wrestled with the guilt that had she gone first at the light, Mark would be alive. Even as her teacher, I could offer Shara no quick-healing balm to such pain. Would she take comfort from my belief that each of us has an appointed time on this earth?

On Monday morning, as occurs in the wake of a weekend tragedy, some students clustered in the halls, crying audibly, murmuring, holding each other. Others with no idea of the tragedy, walked by, curious, whispering questions. It would be a day for hard learning.

Students of the arts often see their band, chorus, or drama room as a refuge in times of trouble. In tragic situations, I have witnessed core-subject teachers offering their students grace to join with other mourners in their elective classrooms. On that day, as my classes began, I suggested that students bring their chairs from their desks, move to the performance area of our room and circle up. I let them talk, ask questions, clarify rumors, and grieve.

At alternate moments, my young almost-adults reminisced and laughed at funny backstage antics they'd shared with Mark, and then all would sink in overwhelming silence. Some hung their heads, a few sniffled, and more than one wounded cry rose up, "It just doesn't make sense!"

A counselor stopped in my room, stood close to the door, and observed the mourning circle. I happened to be telling them that my faith helped me most through loss and sadness; I trusted that the God I worshipped had a greater plan than we could understand. Without quoting the scripture by chapter and verse, I paraphrased one of my favorite Psalms: *"For you formed my inward parts; you knitted me together in my mother's womb."* [1]Everything about each of us is known by Our Creator, including the moment of our birth, our death, and every breath in between. I acknowledged not everyone believed as I did, but that it gave me comfort and a sense of trust. I said little more, afraid that in public school, I had crossed the line.

One of the boys spoke up, "Mrs. Jardin, he went to the altar call at his church just a couple of weeks ago." Several students nodded to one another. Someone said, "He was so excited. He knew he was saved. He believed Jesus's promise of eternal life."

The counselor smiled, nodded to me, and stepped out the door. Later, when we passed one another in the hall, she said, "You know, I figured you had everything under control in there when I stopped by. You looked like you didn't need help from me."

"I didn't know if I was in trouble for speaking about my faith," I said, "but I felt like I needed to be real with my kids."

"Some of them may have needed that," she said as she

left me with another sorrowful smile and moved on. The bell sounded for class change.

I stood by my door, monitoring the flow of students changing classes, some self-possessed, moving with a purpose toward the next test or oral presentation; some shuffling along, papers half-falling from textbooks, still yawning at ten o'clock on a Monday. A gaggle of girls appeared to be comforting one another, as one muffled her cries, hand pressed to mouth. In this stream, surrounded by youths learning new concepts every day in seven different subjects, I, too, was learning new confidence. Two years after the hurricane, in the presence of my students, I could admit Jesus was my Comforter and Counselor.

I had studied the Gospels, translated: *Good News*, all portraying Jesus Christ's life and ministry, showing the Son of God as a compassionate and caring human. In all manner of miracles, He traveled with his followers, healing illness, restoring sight, exorcizing demonic spirits from those possessed, and in more than one instance, raising the dead to life.

In the Gospel of John, upon learning that Lazarus, Jesus's friend and brother of Mary and Martha, had died, more than once the Lord is described as *deeply moved*. As they went toward the tomb, each of the women, at different moments, told him, *"Lord, if you had been here, my brother would not have died."* In simplest terms, we learn of Christ's humanity: *Jesus wept.*

With doubters all around Him, He ordered that the stone lying against the cave crypt be moved and prayed aloud, *"Father, I thank you that you have heard me. I knew that you always hear me, but I said this on account of the people standing around, that they may believe that you sent me."*

Then in one of the most famous scenes from the New

Testament, "*...he cried out with a loud voice, 'Lazarus, come out.'*"

...The man who had died came out, his hands and feet bound with linen strips, and his face wrapped with a cloth. Jesus said to them, 'Unbind him, and let him go." [2]

In school that day, at last, I discovered the presence of His Spirit as grieving and consoling Savior. We knew Mark was not going to be restored to earthly life. For believers, the life promised is eternal: "For God so loved the world, that he gave his only Son, that whoever believes in him should not perish but have eternal life." [3] There is consolation!

Not all miracles we desire will be fulfilled, as the prophet Isaiah writes, "For my thoughts are not your thoughts, neither are your ways my ways, declares the Lord." [4] Yet the Bible bears truth that once was seen by eyewitnesses in towns across the Holy Land, such as Bethany, near Jerusalem, places we can still visit over 2,000 years later: Jesus cares for those He loves and laments with them. And sometimes, miracles still happen when it is the will of the Creator.

I cried at Mark's funeral. Tears flowed for his family and for my own. The faces of Seana, Krissie, and Jimmy drifted through my thoughts, over and over, as I prayed to never have to be *that* Mom. Our boy was almost 13; then they would all be teenagers. So many dangers lurked around their young lives–temptation to experiment with drugs, careless sex, alcohol–how could I not worry? And then, there was danger for the innocents found in the wrong place at the wrong time. Surrendering them to the Lord of Life, trusting His plan, was the only answer.

I still shake my head at the irony. This time, "vehicular homicide due to driving under the influence," wasn't blamed on a sixteen-year-old good kid making a bad choice on a prom night.

With a silent assurance, I let him go: "See you in God's spotlight, beautiful boy."

Refined and Re-Defined

For everything there is a season, and a time for every matter under heaven: a time to be born, and a time to die; a time to weep, and a time to laugh; a time to mourn, and a time to dance;

~ Ecclesiastes 3:1,4-5

Florida Trip, 1994

The weight of loss was still fresh and hard. Two summers after the hurricane, pulled by the same need to remember, the same hunger that draws families to cemeteries and roadside crosses nestled in weeds and wildflowers, we stood in the ruins of Homestead Air Force Base.

We weren't looking for trouble. We'd taken a gamble approaching the main gate. Would we be allowed to enter without "official business," we wondered? The guard waved us through, thanks to an official windshield sticker designating Roy's active military status. The roads were clear, demolition signs were posted about. The desolate land was a ghost town. Gazing out of our car windows, we remarked how strange the 360-degree panorama still included no tall trees.

As we passed a section of base housing, woefulness welled up afresh like ground water. "Playthings" of the wicked wind–overturned rusty barbecue grills, leaning swing sets, dented washers, dryers, and refrigerators–still

189

littered back yards. Continuing into our old neighborhood, we saw that our house number was spray painted with the phrase: "TMO completed 10-18-92." Shortly after that date, the Transportation Management Office had ordered the moving company to deliver the last salvaged items to our new Woodbridge home.

Odds and ends lay scattered in the carport. Now, useless things. Relentless Florida sunshine and humidity bleached white the once sky-blue upholstered couch, and Seana's mahogany dresser, a relic from my childhood, was the color of old bones. I was surprised at the wave of sadness at seeing its carcass. I thought I had let it go the week after the storm. Turning one's back on devastation and walking away does not erase one's history.

Seana and Jimmy were eager to make this return trip to the base, but Krissie preferred to reconnect with an old school chum still living in South Dade County. Not long ago, I asked her why she wasn't with us that day. She said she just didn't want to see it. Perhaps our recovery video had shown her all she needed to see.

My oldest scooted from the car as soon as we pulled into the driveway and went straight to the dresser, pulling each drawer open. Empty. Always outwardly stalwart, she said nothing about it and moved on, begging to go inside the house. Jimmy seconded the motion. Roy and I realized that this was the first time they had seen first-hand the base and our house since before Andrew made landfall. We hadn't promised them a re-entry but keeping their curiosity at bay was impossible.

"Okay," I told them. "But be careful where you put your feet and don't touch anything."

A security policeman in his service vehicle stopped in front of the house. He got out of the car and sauntered toward Roy. "You all can't be here," he said.

Roy was polite, but explained, "This was our house."

Half-smiling, the cop was friendly, but firm. "Yeah, well, technically, you are trespassing … this is government property."

We called to the children to come out immediately. The house was never ours, having been on an Air Force installation, but his words still sounded strange: "This stuff out here is off-limits. County owns it." He trusted we would comply, returned to his vehicle, and drove out of sight.

But until that moment, wasn't it our "stuff?"

Hard to admit to ourselves but nothing in that carport had a place in our lives any longer. We were lingering, staring at lifeless shells left by a mighty tide on an asphalt shore. Hadn't we already gathered the ones worth keeping? I felt a vague pang of letting go all over again and nodded acceptance. Our pilgrimage to this abandoned shore was over. The policeman's official words: "Off limits," seeped slowly into my soul.

Thomas Wolfe famously wrote, "You can't go home again." [1] Truly, there is no going back. "Home" doesn't stay the same. Neither do we. Mistakes, fumbles, scarred hearts are not repaired by pacing back and forth, replaying our past on broken ground. What an act of self-inflicted pain! Maybe our child caught in the middle, sixteen-year-old Krissie, was already gifted with wisdom and insight I was still acquiring. As she processed our losses in her way, perhaps she had already realized that Homestead Air Force base was a wasteland and a squandering of our precious vacation days spent in South Florida. She needed the lifeforce of connecting with friends at that time. Dead things and dead places had no appeal.

But our Andrew story would lie deep in her cache of powerful memories. Deeply intuitive, gifted with a lively imagination and love of words, inspired by a charismatic fifth grade language arts teacher, Kris found a passion for writing stories. I still treasure a poetry collection she published in college. Years after the hurricane, she created an on-line space for authors of faith-based articles, followed by publishing two devotionals for seasons of Lent and Advent. How excited and honored we were to see our church order copies of her first book for Sunday School classes!

In early 2020, just as a new and frightening pandemic seized the attention of the global community, Kris was launching her newest book, *Everything is Yours, How Giving Your Whole Heart to God Changes Your Whole Life*. Poring over her inspired writing, Roy and I tasted bittersweet pride in her accomplishment mixed with lament over the unfortunate timing of publishing in a world distracted.

In a chapter of her newest work, she chronicled the storm's impact on her faith, and that of our family. Her words reminded us of holding fast to faith in loss: "We had to endure being broken by the storm and learn to live on the other side of it before we would ever discover this one invitation that came through devastation. We had to come face to face with our cracks and stare down into the pit of our various holes. We had to accept the refining that comes when circumstances press us out to the edges of ourselves.

"This is what resurrection looks like – God tenderly picks us up from the ashes. He lifts us up from the rubble, and gently puts us back together-but not as we were. The pain that has refined us is re-defined." [2]

The gift in the "ashes" is our ability to raise our eyes toward discovering something better or more lasting. Turning away from the hollow house for the last time allowed me to travel closer toward the Holy One who holds all we own, from the first tiny blanket swaddled around us at birth to the last shroud laid over our faces at death. And then, after letting go of the things of earth, we can rest from our striving, fully His.

We drove out of the main gate that day, allowing the pain its place in our history. We left the remains of Homestead Air Force Base, grateful we could return to the new lives begun in Virginia. But clouds there had already begun to gather, heralding another coming storm. This one was no hurricane. But for our old friends, the Scott family, on the James River shore, their tumult had been building for many years. We could do nothing to keep it from them, but we could do what friends do. We would bow our heads against the tempest, hold them tight, and pray for mercy as their lives were "re-defined."

· §§§

Northern Virginia

Remember, I believe in no coincidences. Air Force Personnel Management could have stationed us on the other side of the world post-Andrew, but it didn't. A three-hour drive separated us from Diane, Richard and Jennifer Scott. The season for mourning had arrived. Kindred spirits needed to be close to one another.

Before we transferred to Turkey in 1988, Jennifer, Kris's playmate, had been suffering from the early stages of Niemann–Pick disease, a rare genetic disorder that usually victimizes children and takes them before or on the brink of adulthood. Attacking the central nervous system, it leaves its victims suffering from neuromuscular failure and impaired cognitive abilities, similar to symptoms of adult onset of Alzheimer's disease.

In the first few years, signs of Jen's disease had been subtle: awkward body movements, including falling beyond toddlerhood, and a distended belly due to liver enlargement, with inability to process cholesterol. Diane and Richard confronted the diagnosis with the determined resolve of warriors, learning everything they could about the cause, history, and the grim prognosis. They were in a race to find treatment for their daughter, working with the National Institutes for Health as it studied Jennifer's case. Her parents devoured volumes of case studies and scientific facts about Niemann-Pick, Type-C, which affects only an estimated 1:150,000 people in the world. But while the diagnosis was spinning their world off its axis, they were treating Jennifer to the most enjoyable life she could live. Like Thoreau, Diane and Richard focused on "sucking all the marrow out life" for their only child, traveling as they were able and enrolling her in the Make a Wish Foundation, created to grant a wish and give hope to each critically ill child in the program.

In 1991, a year after our return to the U.S., we could see the progression of the disease when the Scott family visited our base house at Homestead. While we frolicked at Matheson Hammock Beach, I ached at the contrast between our pubescent daughters. Krissie was lithe and strong, into volleyball and soccer. Jennifer was losing speech clarity and could only walk with assistance.

Eager to treat our friends to interesting sites during their visit, we piled everyone into the station wagon and toured historic Vizcaya, a Miami tourist staple. The early twentieth century estate, built in Italian Renaissance style, featured tours for those interested in the museum, and the European-style gardens and grounds afforded children a place to scamper about, while the adults attempted to fan away the tropical heat.

On that sweltering day at Vizcaya, Dad, always happy to spend time with his grands and their friends, sat with

Jennifer, while our children completed their discovery of the famous landmark.

From a distance I saw under dappled shade, two tired souls keeping one another company: a white-headed man in his seventies, hands on his big pale knees, smiling, leaning in to stimulate conversation, while a pre-teen child sat quietly beside him. He later admitted to me his heartbreak at seeing my friends' daughter, no longer able to speak clearly or keep up with her childhood playmate.

Each of them would soon leave us. Jen knew nothing of her future, while Dad was reporting regularly to his oncologist, picking up prescriptions for transfusions and progress reports on his leukemia. He knew well he didn't have much time left to listen to the mockingbirds' medleys or point out the peacocks' fanning, iridescent blue-green brilliance, gliding in and out of lush tropical foliage and shadows under the banyan trees. But time given was time to treasure.

Dad could make conversation with anyone, anywhere. It was one of his gifts, an amiability by which he learned about a person in a very short time. After a brief interview and laser-focused listening, Art Best could list an acquaintance's birthplace, family, schooling, and ambitions. I can still see him smiling, chatting at little Miss Jennifer Scott, while I am sure she wanted to get out of the heat and spend more time with Krissie. But she grinned back at the old man, nodded, squinting in the summer light, and patiently waited for us to come back.

In less than four years, she would become bedbound. During those years, rapid progression of the disease, as predicted by the doctors, was breathtaking. When Diane called me, distraught after the terror of her child's first seizure, I sat with my back against the wall on the floor of my closet. Listening to the cry of her momma-voice, I ached with her in helplessness.

In 1995, Jen went to the Intensive Care Unit of a nearby children's hospital. Roy and I took time off from work and raced down to Tidewater, Virginia, to be close to our devastated friends.

Because the Scotts called us "family," we were permitted to tiptoe in to see Jennifer. The truth of her condition was clear, even as I could hear Diane expressing hope that Jennifer would go back home. Machines were doing all the work for her fourteen-year-old body. Although the child's eyes were open, they were dull and unfocused. Her gaze turned away from us, from this world. Not one of our prayers would stop time.

Within a few days, my "other" sister and her husband lost their only child. I was stunned that Jennifer was gone so soon. A part of me always hoped somehow, someday, her illness could be reversed. In my grief, I thanked the God of no coincidences for moving us close enough to rush back to hold onto them as their world cracked apart.

For my children, it was a milestone: the first close encounter with the death of a "family" member. Times spent together, frolicking on the river's shore, picnicking, licking birthday-cake icing off their fingers were the stuff of cousin-love. Now they tasted the bittersweet cup of all humankind.

Even as we hurt under the heaviness of grief, faith in eternal life offers a whisper of comfort. Diane asked me to speak about Jennifer at her funeral. "Of course," I said and then sat down on her guest bed, weeping. How would I be able to do it? How could I speak without coming undone, sobbing through my words? A eulogy is the best-worst assemblage of public words. Gathered families at her service deserved reminders of Jen's joy, her feisty, playful spirit, not sorrow over a disease that stole her life.

Diane and I talked about her daughter as we moved about her room. My friend admitted that the canopy bed ruffles and pastel country hues were more of the mother than her late child. Jennifer found energy in bold crayon bright colors and her large collection of books. She especially liked Shel Silverstein's *Where the Sidewalk Ends*.

I cannot say why my children didn't own a copy of the classic children's poetry collection. My drama students, performing oral poetry reading, had introduced me to the poet's whimsical, sometimes hilarious verses. I have since found it one of the most playful books of poetry I know.

I poured over the book and saw the poems I had heard my students read. But I was unacquainted with the one that touched me most: "Somebody Has To." The opening line, "Somebody has to go polish the stars," struck me. Even if literally, we all know we do not leave this world to improve anything, I loved imagining our loved ones looking down on us from Heaven each night, through that twinkling field, "polishing the stars," to keep them bright. What a joyous picture the poem inspired, as I read it aloud over and over! A vision emerged: darling Jennifer Leilani, healed in body and spirit, her once long, dark braids shining, flying out behind her, while she bounded through a field of stars, waving a polishing rag over her head. Jennifer Scott, champion of "capturing the flag."

I begged God to give me the right words to honor this child's brief flash of light in our world. And I trusted He would hold me together when the words came.

My prayer was answered. Strength filled me when I needed it most, to again speak to mourners, reminding them that ours was a Lord of Salvation. Jennifer was gone for now but would be awaiting the rest of us. As I looked over the upturned faces of her loving, hurting family and friends, into the solemn eyes of my own children, our Father gave me the confidence to proclaim that our faith promised a resurrection.

§§§

For many years since the Virginia "tours of duty," we have traveled to share life with the Scotts. "Auntie Diane and Uncle Richard" have continued to celebrate graduations and weddings and other grand family events. For a season, whenever I was with Diane, I wrestled with vague guilt, as though a facet of our friendship had broken away, like a chip of a precious stone. We were no longer able to share the silly things our children did and said, the birthday parties, or the lessons they were learning at school. At times, tormented by not knowing what to say, or how to let her know that I could hardly imagine how her grief sliced into her very bones and soul, I feared we were losing touch.

Late one night, tossed by the storm-tide in my heart, I scratched out a first draft of a poem to her. For years, the scribbled copy lay tucked it into one of my bedside journals. I could not share it with her. I knew that the Spirit of God was responsible for bringing her to a place of rest and refuge. As her dearest friend, I had to accept I was not able to provide solace for her shattered heart.

At last, a time came to offer her my words:

To My Old Friend, Whom I Can Never Comfort
I thought about calling,
Wishing I could give you the joy of talky-talk
Like chuckles of a tireless brook.
Do not mistake my silence for distance.

When I think of the bitter cliffs you climb,
The stone you trace with mourning fingers,
Do you know what tremors pass beneath
The sunny landscape of my face?

Traveling beside you, I grumble about
The flight of my living children
Before I measure the pain
My echoes may cause

What plummets you must suffer,
When I stumble over my little losses.
How you'd give your blood
To have my pebbles under your feet!

We sat side-by-side, before my poem went out to the world. I asked her permission to give it wings. My heart-sister gave me her blessing. Then, as good friends sometimes do, we shared our tears.

Where was Our Son?

*Behold, your father and I have been searching for you in
great distress.*

~ Luke 2:48

Woodbridge, Mid-Nineties

The fear that seized me came up from quaking knees,
grabbed my gut, and sent a chill across my scalp. For an
instant, I felt faint. I stood on the stoop of the house across
the street. Our Jimmy was supposed to be inside, playing
with his friend, Jonathan. His mother gave me a blank look.

"Lord," I prayed silently. "Please, dear God, no more.
We've been through so much, Jesus."

"I thought he went home," Jonathan's mom said. She
could read my face. "Jonathan went with his dad to the
store. I'll ask him when he gets back if Jimmy said
anything about going to someone else's house."

Perhaps I thanked her. I flew across the street trying not
to panic. No, I thought. Our children did not do that. They
never vectored off the path without saying something to us
first. At least, not that we ever knew. . .

I raced up the stairs to his room. Empty.

Bounded downstairs, flung open the basement door and
called down, "Jimmy-Jim?" He didn't make a habit of
hanging out there. In the shadows, only the air
conditioning unit hummed.

The doorbell rang. Jonathan was on the front step, the

201

aura of sundown filling the space behind his dark, closely cropped head.

When I opened the door, he smiled shyly, his small brown hand rising in a small wave. "Hi," he said. He certainly was calm. "Mom said you couldn't find Jimmy. He was at our house, but then said, 'Oh man, I've got youth group!' And he left!"

"Left?? You mean left for church?"

"Yes, ma'am." The little smile curled again. "He was running."

I thanked his best buddy for the news. For a moment, I watched him trot back across the street as dusk settled. I pondered this unexpected report.

Youth were not yet carrying cell phones. I couldn't call Seana and ask for an update on her role as her brother's keeper. The neighborhood streets to our church were quiet. I was reassured that if Jim ran up the half-mile hill to join the youth group, then he must have made it safely. He was twelve, after all.

By the time I was his age, I am sure I had been told one of the Bible's most vivid stories about Jesus as a missing child. Always one of my favorites, the account, in the Gospel of Luke, tells us a little about the relationship between the boy Jesus and both his parents. Having just attended the Festival of Passover in Jerusalem, Jesus stayed behind to sit among the teachers at the temple "listening to them and asking them questions," while his parents started home to Nazareth. They had already traveled a day and suddenly realized he was missing. Perhaps the young boys hung together in the caravan, because children then, as now, find their parents' dull and grown-up talk boring? How did Mary feel when she and Joseph suddenly realized their son was missing? (I think I know!) Jesus's reply was

"Why were you looking for me? Did you not know that I must be in my Father's house?"

Joseph and Mary did not understand the significance of these words, but the episode concludes with Jesus continuing down to Nazareth, "submissive to them. And his mother treasured up all these things in her heart." [1]

Yes, a mother does treasure such things. I knew the relief of realizing Jimmy left running, hungry. Whether for fellowship with other young people also craving more Jesus, or for the joy of lessons and play at a place he trusted, it didn't matter. He was with caring and knowledgeable adult leaders. I could breathe again, and we would talk about improved communication when he got home.

§§§

Years after, Jimmy became our "Captain James Jardin, U.S. Army." As he prepared to return home from deployment in Iraq, I received a surprise phone call. A stranger's voice identified himself as Reverend Werner, the pastor of a Presbyterian church in South Carolina. James, due to separate from the service, had applied for a position there as a youth pastor. Pastor Werner knew our son had been leading his fellow troops in worship with his voice and guitar but wanted to know more.

"Mrs. Jardin, can you tell me what you believe best prepared him for the role of youth ministry?"

I only had to think a moment. I pictured my leggy kid outgrowing his favorite shorts, racing up a hill, as the sun played "hide and seek" behind our little church.

With a brief catch in my throat, I told him the "missing Jimmy" story. He laughed and, in that moment, illumination poured over the memory. God had been preparing the way for James all his life … before his life.

I didn't share with the pastor the secret memory of a silent prayer I had murmured before I conceived our son.

Early in the year Jimmy was born, I lost an early pregnancy. I hadn't yet bought the new, trendy "at-home" pregnancy test, but my cycle was never late. Overdue, breasts prickling, I had been down this road twice. Another baby! My body sang its first notes of silent hallelujah.

Shortly after, wrenching cramps rolled in, a roiling surf pounding my hopeful shore. What I saw through my tears when I miscarried, assured me that truly, a new life had begun in my womb. A little soul, lost. Other than sharing the event with Roy, who comforted me, but had not yet had time to become emotionally invested in my pregnancy, I kept my sorrow to myself. There was no time to grieve. My head was whirling with a pending move to Italy, in caring for two little girls, aged four and two, and teaching middle and high school English classes for several more months. But I began to pray to the God with whom (in those days) I rarely spoke, the God who sometimes granted favors.

As a freshman in college, I once dreamed of giving birth to a fair-haired son. I wrote in my journal that the image was clear, the baby appeared several months old, with light eyes and a dimpled smile. In a love letter to Roy, I told him about the dream and then for several years, put it out of mind. Two beautiful daughters later, we believed we were done with growing a family, and I chalked up the vision to strange things we think about when we are in love, daydreaming about marriage.

But, in a moment in 1981, on my knees at the Base Chapel in Valdosta, Georgia, I asked our Heavenly Father to grant us a son. I promised that I would raise him up to honor His Son, even if asked one day to let go of him as Jesus's mother Mary had done. The gravity of that promise made me tremble. Having recited many a "rote" prayer, chanting "Hail Mary's" and "Our Father's," devoid of true devotion, my supplication poured out my heart, sincere and weighted with sorrow.

It came as no surprise that I soon purchased my first (and only) home pregnancy test and had the joyful result verified at the Moody Air Force Base clinic. Counting the months ahead, we agreed that the season of Advent seemed the perfect time to have a baby. Our James Arthur, robust at nine-plus pounds, came squalling into the world in Northern Italy, two weeks before Christmas.

After the flush of his newborn skin faded and his black "birth" hair fell out, replaced by dark blond, I smiled up at Roy one day while our Jimmy nursed, and told him, "He looks exactly like the baby I saw in my dream."

I never dreamed, though, our son would one day turn away from play and run toward church, our "Father's House." Even more surprising, it had never occurred to me that the boy that I prayed for would grow to be a man devoting his life to leading others toward Christ. We had never urged him to consider ministry. The call was not ours to make.

James got the fledgling pastoral position in South Carolina and continued to seminary with his wife, Leah and three sons. After a few more years, and another move later, he was ordained as a pastor in another church. Seana and Kris, mentored and inspired by the same youth leaders who had also influenced their brother, grew to deeper faith as they matured. The ever-widening ripples from our past continued to carry our family closer to the heart of God.

New Destinations and Detours

As long as I dwell on my own qualities and traits and think about what I am suited for, I will never hear the call of God... The majority of us cannot hear anything but ourselves. And we cannot hear anything God says. But to be brought to the place where we can hear the call of God is to be profoundly changed.

~ Oswald Chambers *My Utmost for His Highest*

Ft. Walton Beach, Florida, 1996-1998

The two of us didn't often get away together. Suddenly, we needed a flight back home to Virginia – stat!

Roy's next position was as the new Supply commander to Special Operations at Hurlburt Field in the Florida panhandle. This meant supporting deployments of highly trained troops to destinations he could not talk about. He was thrilled. We flew down to Ft. Walton Beach together to check out the area. No discussion yet about returning to "hurricane country."

We had a different crisis on our hands.

"Mrs. Jardin, I'm calling because I thought you and Mr. Jardin needed to know I had to take Kris twice to the PRIMUS clinic, yesterday and this morning." I cradled the phone against my cheek and waved at Roy across the Visiting Officer Quarters room. He had just slipped on his beach shoes.

The voice of the young woman chaperoning Kris and

Jim in our absence continued: "The doctor at first thought she had asthma and gave her an inhaler. Now, he thinks she might have pneumonia."

We were scheduled for one more day in the sun-sparkling beach community, eager to survey our next assignment. A flurry of phone calls followed, including speaking to our ailing daughter. Her faint voice frightened us both. Roy halted our brief visit and scheduled a flight back into Dulles the next morning, thanks to the airline changing our reservation due to "humanitarian needs."

"We'll be coming back as fast as we can, sweetheart," we told Kris. No airspeed was fast enough.

When we arrived at the Woodbridge house, we greeted the chaperone and raced upstairs to our daughter's room. We were surprised by the scene.

At the foot of her bed, leaning forward in a chair, his elbows resting on his knees, hands clasped together, was Kris's boyfriend, Kurt. Kris looked up at us, from a nest of pillows and blankets, her eyes underscored by shadows and tearing up with relief. According to our visiting guardian, Kurt had been sitting with her most of the day. Although they had been dating for several months, this was the first glimpse we had of our quiet, gentle future son-in-law facing adversity. Not knowing if Kris's illness was contagious, and unable to help in any other way, he just wanted to sit with her and be her comforting companion. This was a devoted and compassionate eighteen-year-old. We were from that day, completely won over.

Kris did not have pneumonia. For several days, two negative mononucleosis tests gave us nothing conclusive from the local military satellite clinic. Alarmed, we watched her dropping weight and barely able to drag herself out of bed. She was in the last month of her senior year. We asked our All Saints Church family for healing prayers. But we needed earthly assistance too.

Roy was determined to get some medical help, even if we had to travel to Washington D.C. or Baltimore to get it. "If the President of the United States can go to Bethesda Hospital, so can my child," he said.

And so, she did. The three of us made the two-plus hour trip to seek a second opinion.

The young doctor fresh from Naval medical school was interested in Kris's case, because blood tests showed high liver enzymes, yet he didn't see mono. The interview with the three of us, parents with teenage daughter, turned intimate.

Looking at Kris, he asked, "Do you know if you have been exposed to hepatitis?"

She shook her head, "I don't think so."

He continued, "Could you have AIDS?"

I braced myself. How awkward was this for our daughter?

"No," she said, her eyes wide.

"Whew!" Two parents exhaled in silence. In that time and place, neither of us was emotionally prepared to face the conversation that might have followed.

"Well," said our physician, "I'm going to do a deeper dive with a more expensive mono test–going into the DNA. Sometimes the rapid tests don't tell us everything we need to know. I'm almost certain, based on your symptoms, you have a raging case of mononucleosis."

His framed medical degree had not even gathered dust, yet our youthful and qualified physician was correct. At last, confirming what we suspected, Kris could begin a recovery, understanding why she had lost thirty pounds in the month of May and hadn't the energy to do home-school work. Her doctor's orders: "Rest, eat, and rest more."

In the high school conference room, her teachers assured us that she would complete the year "Homebound," without exams and accepting her current grade point average as her final grade. Regaining strength through rest, she passed all courses and recovered enough energy and optimism to walk on Graduation Day. Along with visiting family, we rejoiced at her commencement ceremony and made sure she got a heaping, healthy portion of her congratulatory cake.

§§§

Not long after, we had a moving van parked at the curb again.

"I thought you never wanted to go back to Florida," I teased my man.

"I know," he said with a slight twist in his smile. "But Special Ops!" He was practically salivating, picturing working with service members whose work was usually done behind a shield of darkness.

Seana and Kris were now "college girls." Seana was happily in her second year at the College of William and Mary, in Williamsburg, Virginia, with Auntie Diane and Uncle Richard Scott ready to be surrogate parents after our transfer. Kris, along with Kurt, prepped for her freshman year at a small Christian college in Pensacola.

James, graduating eighth grade, was, no doubt, speculating–perhaps for the first time–that he might have been born into the wrong family. Military life had pushed and pulled our children around all their lives, but this time, our youngest nomad felt the sting of losing connections. After all, a guy's world at thirteen or fourteen is about his buddies and growing into his talents. He had blossomed in singing and performing, and like the rest of us, loved our church family at All Saints. I reminded him that his dad and I met thanks to my parents' momentous transfer from

Miami to Hawaii. His experiences in club soccer league, as well as choral music, would help him find kindred spirits in high school. And, to help ease the pain of transition, Florida meant visits to Disneyworld, Universal Studios, and Aunt Carol and Uncle Ralph, plus pool.

Still charged up and bursting with ideas after the Northern Virginia Writing Project, which segued into working toward a graduate degree at George Mason University, near Washington, I entered the Creative Writing program at University of West Florida, as soon as we transferred.

After a short stint as a substitute at Jim's new school, Ft. Walton Beach High, I approached the principal at one-year-old Navarre High School, near our home. I especially hoped to sub for drama classes. Cordial and enthusiastic, she explained that the school had just opened a ninth grade and would add each grade with subsequent school years. She pored over my resumé scrapbook, admiring production photos from five years of directing full-time theatre.

"Well!" she exclaimed, "I certainly would love to start a drama program here next year. Let's get you to the County office."

I almost broke into song.

She gave me the directions to Santa Rosa Schools Administration. Within two to three weeks of my interview, I received a phone call from the principal of Gulf Breeze Middle School, close to Pensacola.

"I have a teacher leaving for the rest of the school year," she said. "Would you be interested in a March to June job in Middle School Gifted English?"

Perfect, I thought. It wasn't Navarre High yet, but it was a different route to the same destination. Certainly, it was a foot over the county threshold. I jumped into the position with both feet in low-heeled, all-day shoes.

Gulf Breeze, one of Florida's tiny little waterside towns, like Navarre, was a half-hour drive and I resumed my prayer time on the way to school. Hurricane Andrew phantoms returned. The year before, a "one-two" punch from Hurricanes Erin and Opal ravaged the coastline from San Destin to Pensacola. I passed the storms' footprints everyday: multi-million-dollar homes floating in Navarre Sound, a string of hollowed out coastal properties sagging on concrete pilings, decorated willy-nilly, as though petulant children had thrown furniture into the dollhouse upon orders to "Go to Bed!" Almost five years had passed since picking up our broken picture frames and deciding which furniture was worth restoring. Area damage resurrected memories we were trying to keep buried, though I was able to listen to the locals' stories with new empathy.

The flesh added to the bones of my Andrew story were under close examination in my evening non-fiction writing class. With emotions and images tripping all over each other in memory, I needed constructive criticism. But some of my classmates' comments perplexed me.

"Your family is too nice to each other– doesn't seem real. … Don't your kids fight and argue? Use some expletives to sound more real."

I had listened as fellow writers a generation (or three) younger read their drafts peppered with plenty of four-letter words. They instructed me that such usage was *trendy* and *edgy*—what audiences *want* in non-fiction. I thanked them for their evaluation but disagreed in silence. Why do I need to cuss to be understood? My conviction is that readers want to hear an author's true voice. (I admit I do stand guilty as charged for muttering "edgy" epithets inside my car as texting drivers drift into my lane.)

A discouraging moment came, though, when the

professor said the panhandle storms were bad, but hurricanes were *not necessarily* catastrophic. (Hard swallow.) Peering down at me over her purple-rimmed half-glasses and making a broad *all-of-us-here-agree* gesture with pen in hand, she summed up her opinion of my story:

"Nobody really wants to read about another downed tree."

Disappointed that her summation of my efforts reduced the work to a verbal snapshot of the post-Andrew landscape, I self-assessed and decided to postpone graduate studies until I could give them more time. With school about to start, along with the inauguration of a fledgling theatre program, I filed my story away, deciding it would just have to incubate. I didn't know it yet, but I was about to begin the job that would steer me off my well-planned life-map. Who plans a detour?

A Few Farewells and Last Flight Out

*Turn your eyes upon Jesus. Look full in His wonderful face.
And the things of earth will grow strangely dim, in the light
of His glory and grace.*

~ Helen Howarth Lemmel

Florida, 1997-1998

Navarre High opened the opportunity to get back to
my first love in teaching. But the theatre program paired
with English and composition courses enjoyed a brief
honeymoon and raced toward a troubled marriage. Student
essays stayed piled up. Rehearsals lasted until 5 p.m. and
dinner needed to be ready two hours later. I never spent as
much time as I would have liked with James and Roy; after
the kitchen clean-up, schoolwork demanded the dregs of
my energy.

Every night, including Sundays, I sat up in bed marking
a pile of compositions or tests until my eyes were floating.
Glancing at my sleeping husband, I turned out the light
at 11 p.m. or later. The whole routine re-started at 5:30
a.m. Didn't I have more energy once? My last full-time
position with an English/Drama schedule had been in 1979;
the drama was all extra-curricular. For a twenty-six-year-
old momma of a toddler and pre-schooler, it was a mere
after-school workout. Almost two decades later, I was non-
stop exhausted.

I waded into my teacher/director role each day, pulled by
an increasing undertow of personal anguish. After school

hours brought the regular updates from my sister. Dad had fallen and broken his leg; his leukemia turned aggressive. A full-time caregiver tended to our mother.

One day, I raced off campus on my lunch break and returned, emotional and distracted. How I hated the sense of helplessness! Nothing I could do–not even pleading prayers–would help keep my father alive. I swung into the school parking lot.

CRU-U-NCH ! Right into the bumper of a truck parked in front of me. I thought I'd put my foot on the brake. The truck belonged to one of our regular subs. Keeping tears at bay, I found him and we returned together to inspect a small dent.

"Ahh," he said with a dismissive wave of his hand. "That's nothing. Forget it."

"I'm so sorry," I replied. "I'm really out of it. My Dad is dying down in Tampa and I can't seem to focus."

He was sympathetic and encouraged me not to be too hard on myself, which opened the floodgate of tears as soon as I ducked into the nearest Ladies' Room.

Battling a toxic mix of exhaustion from grieving, daily rehearsals, loss of stamina to balance the academic versus extra-curricular load, and the advent of an underperforming thyroid gland, I abruptly left school one midday.

In the first-hour class, I had sent a mouthy fifteen-year-old to the office for grumbling and disrupting a literature test session in my classroom and was shocked to see him sent back before the period's end. At least he kept his smirking mouth closed until the bell rang. I spent most of my planning period fuming inside my book closet, deciding I'd been wrong to assume I could still handle the job. With a pounding headache as my excuse, I checked out from the school. I called Roy and told him to *please* come home for lunch, I needed him.

He found me curled up like an injured kitten on the family room couch.

"I've had all I can stand," I ranted. "I can't keep grading papers 'til I turn out the light and wake up, pick up the pile, and start all over again. And I'm sick of trying to raise other people's kids with no home training. I'm NOT teaching anymore!"

Having tossed him that grenade, I'm sure he could see our financial stability, kids' education bills, my grad school loan, all exploding in our faces. His Air Force retirement was looming, with a prospective civilian job opening in Warner Robins, Georgia.

I was still grousing, "When we move, I'll do something, but not teaching!"

Calm, quiet, and treading with care, he asked the Big Question: "Well, what would you like to do?"

I'd been considering options. "I think. . . as much as I've liked setting up our new homes, prepping them for sale and so on, I might want to sell real estate."

I half-expected him to say, "That's not very reliable income." He didn't.

"Then do it," he said. In that moment he reminded me of my dear father. It was also one of the traits that made me fall in love with my husband. He supported my dreams and schemes. Always an encourager.

§§§

My sister had urged, "Come when you can, he's pretty weak."

At Easter that year, Roy and I visited Dad in University Hospital in downtown Tampa. Ever the affable one, he told us funny stories to tell us about his life in the Oncology Ward, including the nurses checking on him and asking him to take out his teeth. Thanks to a lifetime of good dental care and heredity, they were so beautifully shaped and formed, he had to remind the staff he did not wear dentures.

Nestled down in his semi-supine position in a hospital bed, it was difficult to see how much weight he had lost. His thin face betrayed the wasting process. Still, he had an appetite for a vanilla ice cream cone.

"Oooh, that's so good," he said, leaving no time for melting. "You wouldn't believe how they weigh me," he chuckled, smacking his lips. "They slide me into a sling on the bed and pull me up like they're weighing a horse."

I rode the crest of his good humor and kept him buoyed up with all the news about the children we could remember. This seemed to bring him joy, and easing into the acceptance of his last days, he told us he wanted to be sure that his well-worn car went to Kris and Kurt, as he knew they were engaged and needed "a good set of wheels."

Then, brief and wistful, he said, "I'm hoping they'll let me go home. I told Carol not to bring Elizabeth. She wouldn't make any sense of it. It's just too hard."

Hard. Seeing my mother unaware of her husband's impending death.

Hard. Coming to say good-bye and examine my own conviction of Easter's promise of Resurrection.

Hard, in any season, to bend and kiss your parent and say, "I love you," as you linger, knowing this could be the last time.

A flashback intruded in the last moments with my living father: the traveling man with a big suitcase covered with colorful stickers from different countries, driving in and out of our driveway and our lives so many times . . . One warm dusky summer afternoon, when I was a child at play, I waved across the neighbor's yard without pausing to sprint across the grass to welcome him home. That night he told me I'd hurt his feelings. Years later, I overheard him tell someone that the stinging arrival was evidence he had been away too many times. With such frequent disappearances from my daily life, I'd taken for granted Dad would always come back home. This time, though, he would not return to us.

I looked across the hospital room from the doorway. Assured his faith in God had always been quiet, yet deep-rooted and sincere, I encouraged him with the only words I could find: "Turn your eyes upon Jesus, Dad."

And his unstoppable smile broke across his drawn face. "Oh, I do," he choked.

Not "I will," but "I do." Like a vow. A man committed then and now to His Savior.

Have you ever taken those heavy steps toward a chair, a car, or a hospital elevator with your helpless mate, your battle buddy, holding you up? Still replaying "last words" as doors thud closed, an ominous finality, and you feel your full weight dropping, dropping?

I heard it over and over in my head: "I do."

His eyes had already been looking toward those of Christ, whose Spirit sat with him through those last days.

On the first Saturday morning in May, the closing date of my spring play, Carol called while we were sitting at breakfast.

"Dad's gone."

Her voice was hushed, controlled. "He kept telling me last evening to leave hospice, that he was fine. He didn't want anything more. He wanted me to go home, rest, and not fret over him. The nurses told me he called them during the night, told them he was cold, and asked for an extra blanket. When they checked on him at 5 a.m., he was gone."

A Pan Am man who loved people, good times, fine

food (or a tasty sandwich), and exploring the big cities of the globe, he had finally taken his last flight out. His destination this time: Eternity.

When we gathered in Tampa to celebrate the life of Art Best, a spring thunderstorm raged around the chapel near the mausoleum. Perhaps our Creator was not protesting this man's passing but heralding his Heavenly homecoming with fireworks and an angelic drumline. I recalled how my father once tucked me under his "wing," sheltering his nervous little girl, while loving the drama of a booming, spangled sky.

After his service, consoled by cousins and friends, we celebrated that Dad, whose silver-crowned head often bobbed above the crowd in airport terminals, was gifted with his lifelong ebullient personality. Despite so much personal angst, he was a friend to everyone, treating as equals the janitor cleaning a terminal floor, or a visiting "aficionado" of the company, dining in high style.

One of his lifelong friends took my arm before he left the wake. His clutching hand was a road map of bluish trails through old age.

"You know, there was only one thing your father didn't have in his career."

"What was that?" I asked.

He blinked through his tears and held onto me. "Enemies," he said.

In quiet reflection after the funeral, I remembered how silent our family had been about Jesus, except for perfunctory church attendance in the early years of my youth, Dad's brief recitations of favorite scriptures, and our saying "grace," before meals. For some reason I still can't fathom, speaking about the Father, Son and Holy Spirit, was discouraged, as though too private for utterance. Was it fall-out from the phrase: "In polite company, avoid talking about politics, sex and religion"? Why hesitate to speak of the joy and incomparable gift of our souls' salvation on ordinary days, instead of waiting until Easter and Christmas? Wasn't this Savior we claimed to believe in more than an icon in film and on canvas? Were we worshipping an idol or a real God who, as a man, loved the unlovable, taught in parables, toiled over wood as a Jewish carpenter, then dragged the beams of His cross to Calvary to shed His blood for the salvation of us all?

"Greater love has no one than this, that someone lay down his life for his friends," Christ told his followers. [1] Is this not worthy of our praise?

I thanked God for giving me the courage to speak up and remind Dad to hold to his faith to the end. Living through Andrew did that for me. The nurturing of other believers after the hurricane had done that for me. And it would be our church community in the Panhandle who hovered close and comforted us in losing a cornerstone of our family.

But hands raised in celebration came fast on the heels of sorrow. Roy's Air Force career of twenty-two years ended, with customary ceremony, handshakes, and sheet cake. James and I finished the last few days of school. I was certain my high school teaching days were over.

With the transfer to Georgia, I outwardly took on a new persona. What is it about women, major life changes, and hope found through new hair? With a Princess Diana pixie haircut and a bottle of auburn dye, I wasn't "Mrs. Jardin, teacher," anymore. After all, balancing fresh grief with preparation to begin my next profession, I needed to look in the mirror each morning and think: "Renewal."

We would soon be in a new nest, facing its inevitable emptying. Seana's graduation and commission as an Army Second lieutenant and Kris's marriage to Kurt happened within less than a year. For the second time in our marriage, we were leaving Florida. James stayed behind for the summer, working with his best friend on a tourist boat in Destin. He was maturing, doing his best not to complain at another move in two years, but was sad to soon leave his brother in Christ. Sensing his pain, I had not forgotten the sting of my seventeenth summer and the loneliness of a new home with no friends.

This time, though, with fresh optimism and the car radio turned up, I bounced a bit in my seat beside my best friend, the "ex-military" man, as we crossed the Florida-Georgia border. I prayed to God to lead me where I should go, although I had already made *my* decision. Perhaps the music was too loud. Or maybe it was the thunder of another imminent summer storm. Is it possible I missed hearing God chuckle at my determination to change who He'd made me to be?

Pecans, Praise and Prison

Teach me your way, O Lord, that I may walk in your
truth; unite my heart to fear your name.

~ Psalm 86:11

Warner Robins, Georgia 1998-2014

One of the first places I explored in our new Georgia
house was our "safe room." An interior, windowless
bathroom and storage space under the stairs to our second
story satisfied my need. It had been less than a decade since
Andrew. We still told our story to anyone who asked, and
deep in my bones, I admit I didn't trust God to carry us
through another windstorm. I longed for an ironclad faith,
but viscerally reacted with anxiety to occasional tornado
watches and warnings.

Our new Warner Robins home sat on a three-quarter acre
lot in a one-hundred-year-old grove turned subdivision.
When storms blew through our small city, an hour–plus
south of Atlanta, six majestic pecan trees on the lot pelted
our rooftop with nuts in season. In a year or two, we would
know all the finer points about our lovely, shady trees. In
all seasons, we risked being clobbered by large boughs
self-pruning with little or no warning. Down the heavy
branches would crack, swish, and land with a ground-
shaking thump. Happily, the worst loss was a section of our
wooden privacy fence. For sixteen years, we were blessed
with abundance, usually during alternating autumns. Our
families were thankful when "a year of plenty" meant tins

of pecans on their doorsteps in December. We signed our Christmas gift tags: "With Love, from the Jardin Nut House."

§§§

The best aspect of my new career was the satisfaction of helping clients find or sell their homes. Although I was freed from the demands of the structured school day, with its bells, no time for bathroom breaks, and school-related work most evenings, I found the business world tougher than I'd anticipated. Passing the Real Estate course and licensing exam was not the problem. I tackled two practical challenges. First, although I am a "people-person," I am not an instinctive salesperson. Then there was math, the "game-changer," when I'd once considered a career in meteorology (no matriculating at M.I.T.). Happily, calculators and basic arithmetic were my new friends, as I took extra care with buyer/seller settlement summaries. My first few months as an apprentice, I valued help from fellow agents who kept me out of trouble.

I quickly sorted "trustworthy coaches" from "hardcore competitors." My broker placed me with a million-dollar seller and a cheery, supportive mentor, with the film-star power name of Jennifer Jones. Under her tutelage, I won home listings and enjoyed helping my customers. She also became a loyal friend. As with any sales business, referrals are the key to lasting success. Making a name in real estate meant more than having a face on a yard sign.

Roy, James, and I visited a couple of churches, but found our way to a Methodist church offering both traditional and contemporary praise and worship services. The relaxed atmosphere of the "family life center," (a gymnasium) drew us in. The band consisted of a keyboard and guitars. When they found out Roy's musical background, they gushed with praise to have found a percussionist at last. Just what they needed!

At first, although happy for him, I struggled with jealousy–feeling a bit lost as the band seemed to have all the female voices it needed. We had both been singing in choirs since 1993. Roy mentioned to fellow musicians my experience in both church and theatre, but no one mentioned an audition. As the band sometimes played gigs for other churches and events, I followed them like a groupie, with a childish feeling I had been excluded from the clique.

Before we acquired computer-generated visuals, I was given the task of flipping transparencies with lyrics for the overhead projector. I acquired a new nickname: "Flipper." I accepted it as an odd moniker, with dolphins and porpoises leaping to mind, but I got the joke; pleased to be included, I waded into the band. I satisfied my desire to sing with others, robed with the Chancel choir for the traditional service. But at those moments when we arrived for band practice and a chorus of voices would cheer, "Yea! Here's the drummer!" I felt invisible. I should have defused my jealousy by joking back, "Do you guys know how hard it is to handle this guy's paparazzi?"

One evening, at another Middle Georgia church, our band played for pot-luck supper and peach cobbler. No overhead projector was available. As "Flipper," I was beached. The sopranos suggested I join them on a microphone. So, I did.

At the end of the set, they said, "Hey, you *can* sing!"

From that night, not only did the band accept me as one of the singers, but we also soon transitioned to computer projection. Flipper, the transparency-techie, slipped beneath the waves forever. I recovered from the loss of that first job with the band and rejoiced in making a joyful noise.

Still, even among a group of newfound friends who became like family, my lack of confidence in my own gifts ran deep. In my head, I knew envy is a sin, but how could I seize control of my heart? Of course, the drummer is an attention-magnet; he or she provides the heartbeat of the music. From conception, humans are literally hooked into the sound of a rhythmic pulse. (Some of us respond with the desire to dance.)

The timing for a spiritual retreat was perfect. Our desire to know God more only increased with time. The Methodist church has for many years sponsored a four-day weekend to encourage and support Christian growth known as "Walk to Emmaus," with roots in the Catholic Cursillo and Tres Dias movement. Members of our band had participated, comparing it to a boot-camp for energizing our faith.

On separate long weekends we attended all men/all-women events. Each of us came back refreshed by time away, without phones or wristwatches, learning more about our faith through lessons and music, worship, and jovial fellowship at meals. Called "pilgrims," we came to see and know Christ more clearly through those caring for our every need on the weekend journey, just as on the actual road toward Emmaus, two of Jesus's disciples encountered their resurrected Lord and recognized him as they broke bread together. [1] With the help of one of the spiritual counselors, I confessed my insecurities, releasing that brokenness in prayer. Roy and I found the weekend one of the most spiritually uplifting and affirming experiences of our lives.

Not long after, several men of our church invited Roy

to join them on a similar weekend for incarcerated men at a medium security prison in the heart of Georgia. Kairos International also follows the Emmaus experience in giving prisoners a three-and-a-half-day period of Biblically based encouraging talks, treats never served behind bars, such as ice cream and fried chicken, and most of all, caring and willing ears to listen to the sorrows of men who could be spending the rest of their lives imprisoned. From the Greek, *Kairos* refers to an appointed or opportune time– "God's Special Time"–as the prison ministry calls it. Educating, supporting prisoners and their families, offering unconditional brotherly love and forgiveness, bringing Christ in action through His followers is precious time, indeed. The organization's philosophy is "Listen, listen. Love, love."

My husband came home on a late Sunday afternoon after his first weekend, where he'd played worship songs for the prisoners and led a table talk. Sitting by the pool in the fading light of day, he searched for words to describe what he'd experienced. He wept as he recounted listening to the laments of men convinced that their sins were unforgivable: murder, vehicular manslaughter, child abuse, grand theft. Many of them never knew a loving father or father-figure. Many of their families had cut them adrift. No letters. No phone calls. No love. The prisoners believed themselves unworthy of love, asking who was this Jesus who accepts every sinner with a repentant heart and promises eternal life with Him in Heaven?

Roy was profoundly moved to help bring the Good News of Christ's salvation to these forlorn and often hopeless men. For the first time in his life, he said, he felt called to the "Great Commission" handed down in the Book of Matthew to the followers of Christ:

Now the eleven disciples went to Galilee, to the

mountain to which Jesus had directed them. And when they saw him they worshipped him, but some doubted. And Jesus came and said to them, "All authority in heaven on earth has been given to me. Go therefore and make disciples of all nations, baptizing them in the name of the Father and of the Son and of the Holy Spirit, teaching them to observe all that I have commanded you. And behold, I am with you always, to the end of the age. [2]

At this first Kairos weekend, men from our church and others ministered through short talks on Choices, Forgiveness, and the Gift of Grace. I had never seen Roy so motivated to bring the hope of salvation through Christ to those most in need. Not only did he feel called to join the brotherhood, he played music with the other band members, raised funds, and urged church members to help by baking dozens of cookies–which actually were for the warden and guards. He soon became the local area leader and shared with me that he was never afraid of the prisoners while behind the locked steel doors. I admired his decision to minister to the lost.

§§§

While our spiritual growth flourished over the sixteen years we spent in Georgia, so too did our family. In the red clay of the Deep South, rich with cotton-tufted fields, droopy-leaved peach trees and, of course, bushels of sweet paper shell pecans, our harvest years in the "Jardin-garden" were rich, plentiful, and blessed.

One summer, our joy could be heard all over the neighborhood in bagpipes, boombox tunes, and boisterous voices. Friends and family came from far away to cheer and raise a toast to Seana. Following in her father's footsteps, the wee firstborn child who once toddled around in her pajamas and his Air Force cap, came home a decorated Army veteran. Having received her commission upon graduation at the College of William and Mary, she was selected to become a recruiter, right there at the campus. But with only a brief savor of charming Colonial Williamsburg, military orders changed and she was off to the dry tan terrain and tumbleweeds of Ft. Bliss, Texas to train in Patriot missile defense. We not only beamed with pride over her service, but breathed sighs of relief to have her home safe. For two anxious parents, Operation Iraqi Freedom will always be remembered as more than a televised war. Several times over the months Seana was deployed, our ringing bedside phone at 2 a.m. meant the reassuring sound of her long-distance voice.

Once nicknamed "Little Bit" by a fellow officer, our eldest proved true of Shakespeare's famous assessment of tiny Hermia from *A Midsummer Night's Dream*: "Though she be but little, she is fierce." Determined to be a force for our nation's good, fiercely devoted to caring for her troops, Seana would continue her distinguished military career, even outranking her retired father. That is one salute he gladly gives, along with a special prayer of thanks.

We watched as our adult children began to cheer each other's accomplishments and bear one another's burdens. When together, they still tease and belly laugh like the kids in cahoots they once were. Military officer, author, and pastor, they will always be our children, and we will always be grateful that they changed our lives for the better.

Throughout the Georgia years, their marriages and seven grandchildren added extra seats and high chairs at our festive dining table, especially at Thanksgiving and Christmas. Steamy summers rang with childish squeals and little feet splashing in the pool we could never have in our Air Force years. Our cup brimmed full with joy.

I gave thanks to God for the paths he had made for us away from the sorrow and devastation at Homestead. Truly

He had taught us that there can be beauty from ashes, as He prepared us for another season of our lives.

Soft Songs and a Child's Psalm

The ultimate lesson all of us have to learn is unconditional love, which includes not only others but ourselves as well.

~ Elizabeth Kubler-Ross

Georgia, Spring 2005

Why does it come so suddenly? It's been another vanilla day. You are getting in your car at the end of the workday or night shift, ready to collapse on the sofa at home with a comforting cup and perhaps a savory snack. Your hunger is truly a desire to rest from exertion. Then the phone rings and a voice speaks, as though a hand is squeezing a throat.

It's my Roy. I strain to understand as words topple one on top of another. "Pop just called me. Mom is in the hospital. She's had a brain hemorrhage."

Shocking news in our family, our people, collides with us just like that. Suddenly, it hits like a skid on the ice jars the spine or a kitchen knife slips and slices deep. Ever notice when terrible news comes, we often reply: "But I just saw her," or "We had dinner with him last week?" It is as though we expect some divine reminder to make holy each moment in fellowship, as though it is the last together on this earth.

Only a few weeks before, I was in my in-laws' South Carolina living room. Roy's mother, "Benjie," was leaning in, as we sat side-by-side on the sofa, our heads curled close in quiet conversation. Roy and his Pop heckled one another, loud and chuckling as they shuffled cards and played another round of cribbage at the dining room table. Totally absorbed in their game, they had no idea of our "women-talk."

Roy's Mom whispered about Pop: "He's over *eighty*," she lamented. "Do they ever stop?!" Her brief laugh ended like a sob. "And," she leaned in closer, "It hurts, you know." I was at once consumed by sympathy, too much information, and wonder. We were two girlfriends of different generations who could talk about almost anything. Even senior sex.

Benjie was the very opposite of my own mother. Freedom to express such intimacy was why I was closer to this woman than I ever was with Mom. Early in childhood, I realized I was left to learn about human sexuality from almost anyone besides my parents; although Dad received racy calendars with photos of scantily clad Marilyn Monroe and Elizabeth Taylor-types, only adults could peek. Parental references to the subject usually involved spelling S-E-X, and I grew up ashamed of my curiosity, discouraged from asking questions. Even a potential discussion of puberty was reduced to a vague little booklet about *Becoming a Woman*, published by a feminine product company.

But from the first years of Roy's and my relationship, I had been free to speak of almost anything with my mother-in-law, without fear of criticism or failure to measure up to some undefined expectation. She spoke her mind. She was frank, sometimes more direct than I'd like. But she wore no mask. She'd plant her size-six flowered sandals right where she stood and believed in her right to state her opinion, but never insisting that others agree.

Unaware of impending peril, she had warned us of her fate a few weeks before. She'd fallen in front of the bank. Blacked out. As she was a petite, curvy, attractive woman with a penchant for bright clothes and matching costume jewelry, her greatest immediate concern was her physical appearance. She hated having a broken nose and two black eyes.

Medical tests had been inconclusive. Yet her fall sounded a silent alarm.

But a brain hemorrhage. Another storm was coming in. I couldn't let her go yet; Benjie was "Momma."

Pell-mell, we were boarding our two dogs, throwing two or three changes of clothes into bags, and zooming out of Georgia into the coming dark in the midlands of South Carolina. We found Roy's Pop in their apartment, wide-eyed, still stunned. He told us he found her nauseated and dizzy in the early morning. She collapsed to the floor, unconscious, and he called 911. She was in Intensive Care at Lexington Medical Center, three minutes from their apartment.

She had not opened her eyes.

Roy's older brother, Craig and his wife, Betty, and their young adult children, Charles and Sarah, hovered at the hospital. Charles was putting on his bravest face. My niece murmured her childhood nickname for me, "Hello, 'Auny,'" slipping an arm around my waist and staying close. We took turns at Benjie's side. She looked asleep and expressionless, lying in a tangle of equipment cords and lifelines leading in and out of her sheet and blanket. She had had a massive stroke and there was no road out of this devastation.

In a quiet conference room, the family gathered with the doctor, and we listened to her prognosis. She could be kept alive, but with no reversal of the stroke's destruction and no projected quality of life from this point on. Soundless, Pop cried a little and agreed that they both signed Living Wills for just such a time as this.

DNR. Do Not Resuscitate . . . No extraordinary measures to prolong life . . .Weightless words on a document we sign. For some of us though, the papers must be tendered, the gravity of the legal language takes over, and we buckle under its true burden.

The doctor waited as we foundered in this flood. None of us wanted Benjie, whose personality would be best described as "sparkling," to lie in a bed with a feeding tube, but no brain activity. I leaned into my husband's side, wondering if I was as heavy against his arm as I felt.

Much of the hospital time blurred in tear-stained memory, but I can never forget the last hours holding my mother-in-law's limp hand. Roy and his Pop needed to take a break and I offered to stay with her. I wanted to give her something, a parting gift. She had always been so generous to me, not only with things, but with herself, like the last night in her living room, teaching me the trials of post-menopausal womanhood.

I began to hum music she would recognize from her church services, along with the melodies we sang with our praise band at home. I didn't care if the nurses heard me. Over and over in these years since the hurricane, God continued to lend me His strength. I sang.

...O for the wonderful love he has promised, promised
for you and for me!
Though we have sinned, he has mercy and pardon,
pardon for you and for me.
Come home...Come home. Ye who are weary come
home.
Earnestly, tenderly Jesus is calling,
Calling, "O sinner come home. [1]

The first day or so, an occasional furrow would sink into her forehead, the wrinkle of a brow that asks, "What's that you said?" Then the soft skin of her face, a beautiful face that did not betray her seventy-six years went blank. She didn't respond when I gently squeezed her hand. The nurses suggested she could hear, but she was leaving us. Always faithful and strong in her love of the Lord, she was drifting home. Her journey, without heroic and fruitless attempts to hold her back, took about a week.

Craig sat with her in hospital through the last days. Then, he told us, she sighed soft as prayer and left us behind.

Now, both our mothers were gone.

§§§

A year and a month earlier, my mom had died. I had let her go emotionally, years before. After our time in Hawaii, I ditched my "Houdini tricks." I'd worked my way out of childhood straitjackets of fear and chains of dread. I invested in something more sensible. Before each visit –riding into the storm I called "Mother"–I chose to board up against the stinging rain and the moaning wind under my parents' roof, wherever they lived.

With a hammer of unforgiveness and a handful of special nails, I slammed up my protection:

BAM! A nail of armor. I was too tough to cave to my mother's tears.

BAM! A nail of distance. Avoiding proximity was key.

WHAM! A nail of distractions: stay busy when she was near. Run a vacuum or run an errand. This nail lay close to "distance."

Braced against harm, I didn't realize until many years later that my "nails" pierced me. Keeping up my defenses, I forgot or ignored my mother's gifts and admirable qualities. When I think of her now, I realize she gave me appreciation of beauty in the world around me.

Mom loved the ethereal elegance of drifting sea horses at the Miami Seaquarium and the funny, big-throated pelicans diving off Key Biscayne. When I was little, as we drove over the bridge to Crandon Park Beach, she pointed out the ibises, swooping terns, and sometimes a rolling dolphin.

Her colors were shades of the ocean and shells. She surrounded herself with a spectrum of blue-greens, coral pink and gold. These hues dominated her design work; and her room interiors were rich with luxe fabrics, from fur to brocade; she added fine woods, unusual art, and accessories often purchased while traveling with Dad to Europe, Central and South America, and Asia.

When not near the ocean, she loved Miami's Fairchild Tropical Gardens and could name all the plants. At the Gardens' annual fair, "The Ramble," she always ended up in the used book tent, looking for more British history, another mystery, or odd collections of poetry. She adored Elizabeth Barrett Browning, Robert Louis Stevenson, and the varied works of Rudyard Kipling. I would find a Nancy Drew mystery or collection of fairy tales. I, too, loved to read. Still do.

The devils of her mental illness had plundered her life. They stole her beauty, crushed her artistic ability, and ransacked her reason. A relentless ache settled over the last years I spent in her presence. When Roy and I visited with the children and she stayed in her bed, my father nudged me to go to her room and check on her, or make small talk, or ask her if she was ready to eat (so that she would not launch into a tirade at him).

My hard-nailed boards in place, I would stand awkwardly a few feet from her bed, wish I could be anywhere else, and try to remain pleasant. Mostly, I wrestled with frustration that nothing between them changed, until her loss of short-term memory wiped away the war, and my father was gone soon after.

Shortly before her passing, my sister, who managed their affairs in the last few years, recommended I try to get down to Tampa to see her in the Alzheimer's care facility where she lived following the death of our father. School was out for summer. Roy and I drove down from Georgia.

In her pleasant daylit room, with a handful of framed family faces gazing on, we found her in a narrow bed, with a blanket nearly to her nose. She was curled up, a wizened child almost lost in the bed. So tiny.

"Mom," I whispered, to rouse her. "Hi, Mom."

A smile drifted across her tightly crinkled eyes. A passing cloud. Did she know my voice?

I spoke again as Roy sat near me, and I put my hand on her shoulder. "Just came by to say hi and I love you."

I said it because I needed to. The words were not for her. They were for me. I knew God loved me, despite all the ways I'd disappointed Him. I needed to do the same for the woman who often had left me adrift in a beautifully furnished lifeboat, while she fought to keep her own sinking vessel afloat.

Her eyes closed again. She no longer could speak.

I struggled to find words. Unlike Benjie, she was not a praise music lover and did not sing. But I knew she grew up with the Bible.

"The Lord is my Shepherd," I began and spoke the first scripture I had memorized in childhood, and half-forgot during the night of Andrew. I am sure that, like the Gettysburg Address, and memorized poems of Longfellow and Frost for English class, I had recited it for her, awaiting her approval. I'd so hungered for it.

I was guiding her now, this disappearing wisp of my Mama, reminding her and myself of God's ultimate grace and care for His faithful. I had no idea of her spiritual journey with the Father through the end of her life. Once, she'd sat beside me in a church and stilled my wiggling with a firm, neatly manicured hand. Her fingers in my hand now were bent and twisted with rheumatoid arthritis.

My husband's hand gently lighted, then stayed on my back. Did she hear me? Did she understand the words and the promise?

… Surely goodness and mercy shall follow me all the days of my life,
And I shall dwell in the House of the Lord Forever. [2]

She passed away a few weeks later. Carol had pre-arranged all details, except for selecting flowers for her. My sister wanted us to select them together: a spray of tropical colors a Miami interior designer would treasure. Only family attended her funeral; then she was laid to rest in a vault in Tampa, beside our Dad.

I can't go back and re-love my mother. But wisdom has broken through my defenses. The protective boards of my younger years never served me well; all lie pale, splintered, and scattered on the road behind me. Tenderly, the Great Healer, who once ripped away boards by storm, has pried mine away. He has loved down my walls. He has spilled His redeeming light over all the broken pieces of our elusive mother-child bond, surrounding me with the soul-nourishing affection of my own children, their mates, and our grandchildren. What astonishing grace is given a sinner like me!

How I would relish the opportunity to sit with my mother now, with her mind restored. I would pour her an English tea or iced coffee, which she enjoyed with a scoop of vanilla ice cream: "A coffee flip," my Dad called it. We would talk about the kaleidoscopic colors of sunset and creative landscaping of our neighbors, in the peace and quiet busy-ness of the creatures around our pond. She would delight in the anhingas, egrets, and the Great Blue

Heron who drops by biding his time, golden eye fixed on the water, awaiting his catch.

The older I grow, the more I see the ways I am like her. For a long season, I grieved over never having a mother's closeness. Had the demons not locked arms around her so early in our lives, we might have also been friends. My prayer is that I will recognize her in Heaven. At first, I'm sure she may look like someone else, for all of her tears will be wiped away. But I think I will know her for her smile, the one that once thrilled and delighted me when I was very small.

A Risk in the Spotlight

Teach and urge these things.

~ 1 Timothy 6:3

Warner Robins, Georgia 2014

The audience's eyes are all on me. I'm uncertain of the exact words I am about to say. But I know they are bubbling up from a stream of faith. What I want to say to the audience before me may get me in trouble. No prepared remarks on an index card in my hand, yet I must speak. After teaching twenty-five years in the classroom, peer education, a decade-plus of long-term subbing, summer school gigs, vacation Bible schools, and Lamaze childbirth training for pregnant parents, I'm ready to make a break for the beach. Before "goodbye," I am compelled to leave one last bit of wisdom.

At first, ego-driven, hungry for acceptance from my students, I'd entered the profession anxious to use the classroom as my stage. I entertained as much as I instructed. After falling flat on my face a few times–usually because I thought I had all the answers–the lights bumped up full on my life-stage and I realized the gift for teaching was never about me. My students have always been "my other kids." For a brief time, they have been entrusted to my guidance. I cared about each of them as young emerging adults. Two weeks from graduation, my last set of seniors is ready to soar. With pride in their achievements and hope for all those youth God has placed in my path, I now stand ready for commencement, too.

Looking around the theatre, I don't see any administrators. Is it possible my politically incorrect, non-school-board sanctioned remarks will not end my career in commotion?

One of the faces in the crowd is that of my friend of more than two decades, Sheila. In this chapter of our lives known as the "Georgia years," she has been faithful. She and husband, Jim, have embodied true friendship, from sharing short getaways, to always being among the first at our house, for jubilant celebration or prayer in the quiet stillness of grief. We've shared many of the same roles: two wives, two moms, two teachers, and alongside Jim on guitar and Roy on drums, two singers in our church praise band. Through weddings and funerals, crises large and small, our bond runs deep.

We "girlfriends" have walked miles together for several summers at our local mall. Orbiting the myriad of stores, not yet open for shopping, we have exercised our legs and our jaws for almost an hour daily, then guzzled gallons of iced tea through another hour of "cool-down" conversation. Locals have also spotted us at a favorite restaurant, splitting a decadent little slice of chocolate cake to celebrate our birthdays. Healthy friendships need traditions!

She has beat me to retirement by a year. Her field was Elementary Special Education, specializing in Autism. Remember my fright the first time I subbed in an autism classroom, upon learning the absent teacher had been injured by her student? Sheila's life was altered by an angry student who slammed a chair into her knee. Though the same knee later had to be replaced, she has long since forgiven the boy who hurt her. She understood that he was not in control of his outburst. She lives the Gospel message: "Offer forgiveness, as we are forgiven." By her gentle words, prayers, and faith in action, she is one of my life's heroes. Because God put her in my path after Andrew, I am stronger in trusting Him.

Now, she and Jim, several other dear friends, my drama Booster parents, teachers, and students past and present, have surprised me with a Sunday afternoon farewell party in the school theatre. Several of my brightest stars have danced, sung, and presented a power-point of my life, with a collection of pictures Roy has secretly shared with the organizer. (Yikes, I didn't know he'd kept *those*.)

Now, it's my turn to thank them. I need to speak the truth about the last fourteen years that almost didn't happen. Eighteen months into our new chapter in Warner Robins, I could have made a name for myself in real estate sales. With my slick professional photo plastered on flyers and company sale signs, I was navigating my promising new career. My mentors assured me that with years of experience, a conscientious realtor could begin to make a fortune in satisfied customers' referrals. I'd already begun to build a database of happy clientele.

But I'd walked away.

My smiling satisfied "customers" are seated in rows in front of me. This is wealth beyond measure: our labors of love over classroom productions, one-act play competitions, full-length musicals such as *Joseph and the Amazing Technicolor Dreamcoat, Les Miserables*, and *A Christmas Carol*. We've worked nights, weekends, and school holidays on numerous dramas, children's theatre, and classroom plays to entertain an appreciative community. Our audiences' reviews: "You kids are amazing . . . So professional . . . Can't believe we have so much talent here!" There are no paychecks for that. Those who have enriched my life in this season are sitting before me, and I have a bully pulpit.

After expressing my total surprise and gratitude for the send-off, I tell them how I almost didn't return to teaching after 1998. Exhausted and mourning Dad's death, I'd casually dropped off my resumé with James's new high school principal at Houston County High. It was pure muscle memory: move into new community, update the job history and references, drop it by the principal's office, walk away, and wait for a phone call. But I really didn't want it. I had just signed the check for the Real Estate Academy, a new school year had begun, and then up popped a teaching position on Labor Day weekend of that year.

"No, thank you," I told the principal's secretary. "I am currently enrolled in real estate school." Then a compulsion: "But keep me on file, in the event I decide to make a change." Another offer came at semester's end, but I had just passed my license exam. No lesson plans, gradebooks, parent-teacher conferences or fifteen-minute lunches. Thanks, anyway. Call me "Bronwyn Jardin, Realtor."

After two years as a Coldwell Banker associate, enjoying a modicum of success as an apprentice, I ran into an obstacle to my plans. His Name was Jesus.

I tell my audience I believe in the significance of Biblical numbers, such as "three" and "seven, " God is the Trinity: Father, Son, and Holy Spirit. Jesus died and rose from the dead in three days. Creation lasted six days, plus a day of rest. Jesus instructs the Apostle Peter that forgiveness is not granted seven times, but *seventy times seven*.[1] These are the numbers of completeness and fulfillment. Perhaps, I told them, my three invitations to accept a teaching job at Houston County High, were the offer toward fulfillment in my life? I admit I was so shaken after the third job opportunity offered face-to-face by the school's principal, just after James's graduation ceremony, that I wept later to my sister and mother-in-law about the encounter. I had vowed I was *not* going back.

In fact, James had come home after school several weeks before, unknowingly testing my resolve. "The drama teacher is leaving. You might want to check that out, Mom!"

"Oh, no," I told him. "I don't think I'm ready to stop selling houses yet."

Perplexed at this unexpected opportunity, I only knew that for the next few days before going to my interview, I needed to pray, seeking divine guidance. After all, hadn't I twice refused job offers from this school? Shaken, I talked to my Father, Counselor and Savior. I searched for His answers, by diving into Scripture.

I shared with my audience that random reading of the Bible before going for my interview pointed back to teaching. No, this is no guarantee of finding God's Will, I explained, but, in good faith, I was faced with a major decision; so, I searched for holy help. In several passages, *"guiding"* and *"teaching"* leapt from the pages of the Bible, as though God had highlighted the key words. Once again, no coincidences:

For as in one body, we have many members, and the members do not all have the same function, so we, though many, are one body in Christ, and individually members of one another. Having gifts that differ according to the grace given to us, let us use them: if prophecy, in proportion to our faith; if service, in our serving; the one who **teaches***, in each teaching…*[2]

Now you are the body of Christ and individually members of it. And God has appointed in the church first apostles, second prophets, third **teachers***, then miracles, then gifts of healing, helping, administrating, and various kinds of tongues.*[3]

Show yourself in all respects to be a model of good works, and in your **teaching** *show integrity, dignity, and sound speech, that cannot be condemned...*[4]

I confess that when I signed my 2000-2001 school year contract, I was doubtful. After all, in typical rebellion, it hadn't been *my* idea. Remembering the long Navarre High nights and stacks of compositions, I tiptoed back, trembling at returning to English and Drama. I made a mental promise: "One year. I will try it again and quit if I can't handle the pressure." Late in the fall term, spinning in the mix of grading senior term papers while conducting rehearsals for the annual Regional One-Act Play Competition, I requested that I either teach *all* drama or *all* English classes as soon as practical, or resign. Once again, I was overwhelmed with after-hours work.

Happily, our fall One-Act placed third out of eight schools and in spring 2001, and the administration assigned my English classes to another teacher. I won the role of full-time theatre director. Drama and technical theatre classes, all day, every day. The "dream job." And God's surprises weren't finished.

Directing my favorite subject also included exhausting nights and sometimes hard confrontations with unhappy students and/or their parents, whose dreams of starring roles were smashed. One of my toughest responsibilities: measuring and balancing every aspect of each student's gifts, as well as their "chemistry" with others in each production. Despite the disappointments and emotional bumpiness, I prayed over my students, each ensemble cast, and felt guided by the Father's hand. Other teachers and parents shared that they were praying for the success of the theatre program too.

The community grew to trust and support our productions. My gifted fellow artists teaching chorus, band, and art collaborated, and our students witnessed adult teamwork in action. Drama parents built a Booster club and assumed an increasingly active role, supporting a myriad of production tasks—fundraising, building sets, furnishing props, managing costumes, printing programs, feeding large casts on dress rehearsal nights, and running a box office.

Now that Roy and I had stopped moving every two or three years, our roots sinking deep under the pecan trees, I received a first in my lifetime gift: the blooming of a theatre program begun long before I arrived.

Throughout my tenure, some of my audience had heard episodes of my hurricane saga. Sometimes stories had emerged as we slapped paint on sets on weekends or waited for late parents to pick their children up after rehearsal. They know I trust Jesus because I have seen His peace and reassurance shining through dark passageways of my life. Everything I have been given, everything I have to offer belongs to the One who promises my soul eternal life:

Again Jesus spoke to them, saying, I am the light of the world. Whoever follows me will not walk in darkness, but will have the light of life. [5]

I am compelled to tell my audience that Sunday afternoon, "I almost bypassed this opportunity. After all, it hadn't been in my neatly designed plan. But in this, in everything, I've turned my trust over to God. Don't rely on your own understanding," I urge them, "but seek faith in the Creator to see you through your life."

I stop talking. Deep breath. Smiling faces look up at me; some are nodding. Now, they are applauding. I can't

248 A Risk in the Spotlight

remember when I last felt this deep welling-up of joy and hopefulness for my students. These young people, parents, and supportive friends have blessed my life.

No one arrives to tell me I have violated county policy. No administrators are looming in the back of the theatre, waiting to frog-march me to the office to face the consequences of telling my students my faith story, uttering the words *seek God, Jesus* and *faith.* My retirement is safe; this is my graduation day. I am ready to begin my new role: Author.

After a cake and punch reception, swapping memories with alumni, and receiving several precious gifts, including a scrapbook treasure of sentiments from my dedicated thespians, I step out into the late May afternoon light juggling keepsakes and flowers. From the theatre to the car, I walk with my Roy: life-long helpmate, unsung heroic stage-set engineer, and most loving booster. Forty-three years before, no older than these graduating students, he was an island kid who fell in love with a goofy mainland girl, hiding pain behind a mask, taking her bows on our high school stage. Now, I leave the shadow of the woman they have called "Drama Mama" fading into the silent wings. It has been a good run.

Beyond the parking lot and the school grounds, the western spotlight dazzles as it splits the dusky lavender clouds with golden fingers. "God's fingers," I like to call them, pointing us toward Heaven. I'm startled to find my eyes are watering. Such a glorious sundown!

Fear Not, Shore Birds

I must down to the seas again, for the call of the running tide

Is a wild call and a clear call that may not be denied;

And all I ask is a windy day with the white clouds flying,

And the flung spray and the blown spume, and the sea-gulls crying.

~ John Masefield, "Sea Fever"

Florida 2014 – Present

Irresistible. No denying it, Roy and I longed to leave land-locked middle Georgia and return to Florida. After all the military moves and sixteen civilian years in Warner Robins, we never lost our craving to live by the ocean. Once, we were two teens from opposite sides of the country, with sunburned cheeks and sandy feet, saltwater sluicing through our veins. We spent countless hours playing in the turquoise Pacific surf. Now, decades later, as we considered a retirement destination, the tidal pull felt stronger than ever. Overcoming our fear of another hurricane, giddy to be close to the beaches, back we went to Tampa Bay, our place of refuge after Andrew.

As we zipped about nearby Apollo Beach, finalizing our move into a small retirement community villa, a signpost on the side of Highway 41 caught my eye. I stared at a measuring stick of sorts, warning hurricane storm surge could get "this high," a height taller than either of us. I gulped. Battle scars fade, but the memories glide in and out like ghosts. Twenty-two years. I could still be triggered.

"Did you see those hurricane signs along the highway out here?" I asked Roy the next day.

"Bronwyn," he said. "I'm not going to live in fear. If one's coming, we'll close up the place and leave town."

For three years, life on the waterfront was quiet. In September 2017, peak season for Atlantic storms, we decided to purchase a lot and build a larger home. We realized we'd downsized too much with our first retirement nest. We had just staged our little place for sale, rented a storage unit, and stowed two pick-up truck loads of boxes of books, framed pictures, and furnishings. Evening weather reports alerted us to a significant hurricane, perhaps still two weeks away, moving toward Florida and the Gulf of Mexico.

Seana called. Her Army posting at Northcom in Colorado Springs afforded her a look at potential threats to the continental U.S. and Canada. "Pay attention to this storm," she said. We trusted her expertise. Hurricane Irma swelled into a strong and geographical giant.

Soon, public warnings ramped up. Dire predictions suggested a Category 4-5 strength hurricane with catastrophic potential would roar up the center of the state, including both coasts of the peninsula. On a Monday, when we told our realtor to temporarily suspend our house sale, as we were planning to evacuate by the end of the week, she exclaimed, "Why are you waiting? I'd leave tomorrow if I could!"

We agreed she was wise. We would make a Wednesday evening escape to Georgia, following rush hour. Irma was still several days away. On Tuesday night, we shared supper and our evacuation plans with our Pastor Craig, his wife Frances, and friends. In so many ways, we felt like we had come full circle; there we were, back in Riverview, our temporary home after Andrew. Now, we were members of Redeemer Church, only blocks from our refuge with Carol and Ralph in 1992. How perfect our church name, in light of all we had learned about redemption on the winding road that brought us back to where our searching hearts began.

After dinner, grim and industrious, we whirled into preparation, rolling up the area rugs, picking up anything stored under beds or on closet floors, placing precious collectibles inside the washing machine, and gathering the important papers. Photographs, which always rate high on my "save in case of disaster" list, were almost all in the storage unit in downtown Apollo Beach. Many had been replaced following Andrew. Yes, we could live without them, but how I dreaded the thought of "Salvaging Stuff: The Sequel."

On Wednesday afternoon of that week, we closed and locked the hurricane shutters on every window and door. Accordion-style, they could be pulled across windows in seconds and unlocked with a key. They had been expensive, but sturdy and priceless for quick evacuation. Our "seasoned" neighbors had scoffed during the installation, insisting the Tampa area had not had a major hurricane in decades. But now we all braced for damaging wind and water. Those who were unprepared became victims before the storm. It troubled us to later learn that shady handymen swooped like vultures into our neighborhood, offering aid to the elderly neighbors–especially widows–physically unable to screw sheets of plywood to their windows. They demanded exorbitant fees, and fearful residents paid them.

My sister and her husband had already mounted their shutters, when we urged them to evacuate to Georgia with us. Far from flood zones, they decided to remain in their home. Nothing we said could convince them to join us, as waves of post-traumatic stress buffeted the two of us. With trembling hugs and kisses, we parted, and they promised to check on our home as soon after the storm as possible.

In our two cars, we slogged our way north on I-75 toward Georgia in heavy post-rush hour traffic. We slowed to an inch-by-inch crawl, while the Florida Turnpike emptied thousands more on the interstate, residents fleeing the Keys and Miami. Four days before the expected arrival of the storm, bumper-to-bumper evacuees drained the resources of fast-food restaurants and gas stations. Cars and trucks lined the shoulders by rest areas already forced to close.

Thanks to God's providence, we had managed to reserve a hotel room in Lake City, not far from the Florida-Georgia border. The operator told Roy we got the last room available in the hotel's chain that night. Normally the trip from Lake City to Tampa takes two hours and thirty minutes. Our trip lasted seven hours.

Roy and I talked to one another nonstop on our cell phones. Fatigued, I fixed my eyes on a U-Haul trailer's taillights, as traffic moved at a slug's pace. I knew I'd gone into a mental danger zone past midnight, when suddenly a different set of lights had replaced my leading trailer. I couldn't remember anyone changing lanes! Grateful to be awake enough to survive the trip, we fell into the Lake City hotel bed around 3:00 a.m.

§§§

In Georgia, one of our dearest friends, Grace, from our Warner Robins church family, sheltered us for the following night, offering her home to us for the duration of the storm. Her husband, Barry, had passed away the year before; we spent a calming evening of fond reminiscing, then retired early, still anxious and weary after exiting Florida.

I woke bolt upright in the night after evening weather reports had sunk into my brain. From Ohio, our Kris had texted us, "Your rooms are ready." I waited for Roy to wake to share my realization.

"What are we doing staying here?" I whispered to my drowsy man. "This thing is projected to come right up I-75 behind us. We need to help Grace secure her house and take her with us to Kris's. The storm won't have the steam to get to Ohio."

We shared the invitation, but Grace would have none of it. Her own children had been urging her to get to Atlanta as soon as possible to get out of harm's way. Strong and confident, she preferred to ride out whatever remained of the hurricane in her basement.

"You all go on. I understand completely," she said with her sweet Georgian accent. "But I don't need to go descend on Krissie and her family. She is a dear to offer, but I will be just fine here. I have everything I need already. Flashlights, food, and extra water."

With true "steel magnolia" spirit, she was not going to leave her solidly constructed home. Regretting we could not persuade our friend to travel with us, we prayed for her safety, helped move all her outdoor furnishings to secure places and headed north. In her basement-level carport, she kept our second car safe from flying debris. Thankfully, she made it through the storm with only some minor tree damage, far from her roof.

Adrenaline-fueled, Roy and I chatted on the phone with friends and family on the way to Ohio, both of us fretting about having to start over again, remembering the panorama of devastation and lengthy recovery from Andrew. I recalled the warning signposts when we moved into Apollo Beach, in Hillsborough County Flood Zone 1. Would the whole little town disappear into the bay?

I trembled, even *knowing* we are members of God's family, held in His hands no matter what. The memory of one of my favorite passages from the Gospel of Luke, printed in red letters denoting Jesus's words, surfaced:

Are not five sparrows sold for two pennies? And not one of them is forgotten before God. Why, even the hairs on your head are all numbered. Fear not, you are of more value than many sparrows.[1]

If God counted every graying hair on our heads, if He cared for the little birds of the air, surely, He would see us through another storm. In my life-long battle to trust those who claimed to love me, I was again challenged to embrace His promises.

Within a day or two, prayers were answered. While we treasured the impromptu vacation with Kris, Kurt, and four of our grandchildren, news came from my sister. After a much smaller storm than expected, she and Ralph found our home safe and dry — and almost untouched. Our damage: a few broken clay roof tiles. Our town was spared, even of spotty power outages across two area counties.

What relief! But what exhaustion followed several days of reliving one hurricane experience and fearing the onslaught of another. Theologian and writer Frederick

Buechner reassures us, "Here is the world, Beautiful and terrible things will happen. Don't be afraid." [2]

I want to tattoo those words *inside* my body. How faith and fear often have wrestling matches under our skin!

§§§

We still live where hurricanes can track. Six months after Irma, Roy and I were in our new home alongside a pond we have named *NaniKai,* Hawaiian for "beautiful waters." But this time, we chose higher ground.

Before the sheetrock went up in our home, we scrawled onto its bony frame favorite passages of scripture, from Old and New Testaments. No one else may ever see them, but we know they are there:

Unless the Lord builds the house, those who build it labor in vain. (Psalm 127:1)

All things work to the good for those who love the Lord and are called according to His purpose. (Romans 8:28)

As for me and my house, we will serve the Lord. (Joshua 24:15)

We always want to remember that those words are a living part of our foundation.

Our NaniKai is twenty-five miles from Tampa Bay, yet sea gulls and pelicans sometimes dip and glide in the airwaves over our house, evoking the call of the tides. Most days, our companions are Great Blue herons and white egrets, slick black "snake-birds," diving for small mullet, and a shaggy wood stork balancing on one long leg, while raking his long toes in the shallows of our shores. They swallow still-wiggling fishes and avoid an occasional stealthy gator gliding past. Sandhill cranes, eyes masked in flashy red, wander our streets in pairs or with their plain tan colts, sometimes rousing the entire neighborhood with their raucous caws. A tiny grey finch has even made his home in an oak outside our backdoor and frequently darts, then lights on our screen, as though to ask, "May I come in?"

Of course, we are surrounded by birds. Through them, our Creator reminds us daily of His provision. Through sun and scuttling clouds and rumbles of storms, how much more He has shown us His loving care!

Epilogue

Be merciful to me, O God, be merciful to me, for in you my soul takes refuge; in the shadow of your wings I will take refuge, till the storms of destruction pass by... Be exalted, O God, above the heavens! Let your glory be over all the earth!
~ Psalm 57:1,5

It's hurricane season again. The Eastern sky wakes in shades from rosy pink to salmon red every morning. Each day, the Florida heat rises so high, that only a crackling good thunderstorm can provide relief.

Boom! Boom! The eternal concert begins in a cymbal roll of rain across NaniKai pond, dark as slate.

The tempests of my younger years are over. Growing old has allowed me the blessing of learning to give and receive love, forgiving and being forgiven, navigating the rough, uncertain and joyous road of parenting, keeping life in perspective, and trusting that no matter what, the Lord is near.

Years ago, James was home for the summer from Valdosta State. He thumped down the stairs one morning and found me puttering around the kitchen. With a hug and a wide-eyed grin, he said, "That was one cra-a-zy storm last night, huh?"

My face must have betrayed my surprise.

"Didn't you hear...? You DIDN'T hear the thunder?" he continued. "Oh my gosh! It just crashed —more like exploded–over the roof. I figured you probably jumped off the bed!"

Almost as astonished as my son, I looked at my last child, becoming a man. His face was frozen in amazement, his dark eyebrows thick, the image of his Dad's, arched over wide green eyes. Like his Momma, though, he had a flair for the dramatic.

I shrugged and smiled. It was a good, deep sleep. A decade plus, after the real-life drama of Hurricane Andrew, was I finally learning to trust the One who had carried me through countless storms, inside and outside my home, under the bed, in basements, closets, or huddled in hallways?

Sometimes, when clouds boil black over our backyard, I nestle in my cozy tropical floral chair, my front-row seat to God's drama. When the rains come, the drops dance across the surface of the pond like thousands of silver coins tossed in a fountain all at the same time. Flashes of light fly upward from the broken surface of the water. My delight never wanes. "He restores my soul . . ." [1]

With less than a day's notice, Roy and I could be scurrying around to prepare for another storm again. We know the drill: stow away the keepsakes, pull the shutters, grab the "go-bag," and pray our way North. We have chosen to live in this place, knowing that all we have on this earth can be taken from *any* of us at any time. This is after all, only our temporary home. It doesn't have to be swept up by the winds; the foundation may sink beneath us, the walls may crumble to ash, or our possessions may end up in someone else's pockets.

When the strong box holding all our hurts, disasters large and small, is unearthed from within our souls, we cannot examine any order in the bits and pieces of our lives until the lid is lifted and the light spills down. Out of the wreckage, shines the unexpected: shards, splinters, and slivers create the mosaic. What once looked like chaos emerges as divine design. It may take a long time. *Kairos.* God's special time.

In her autobiography, *The Hiding Place,* Holocaust survivor Corrie Ten Boom recalls her beloved sister, Betsie, saying: "His timing is perfect. His will is our hiding place. Lord Jesus keep me in Your will! Don't let me go mad by poking about outside it." [2]

The "hiding place" I'd searched for my life has always been available. Learning to live in God's will is the journey of a lifetime.

§§§

Once, a few years before my retirement, the advanced art and drama students shared a field trip to the High Museum in Atlanta. Featured that day were the works of the Impressionists: Renoir, Degas, Monet, Matisse . . . .

Some of the students stood so close to the masterpieces, they couldn't see the subject. "It just looks like a lot of dots," I heard one say.

"I don't get why this is so classic," agreed another.

I leaned in and murmured, "Move back a few feet. Get some perspective."

We all backed away and some agreed, "Yeah, now I see it." The splashes of color, the dots and splotches worked and played together, their beauty emerging, blooming.

Monet's *Houses of Parliament (London in the Fog),* which I later learned was only one of a series, was my favorite in the room. Even in the painting's murkiness, there is light and reflection in the River Thames. I was attracted like a moth to that light. The farther back one stands, the more the eye is drawn to the twilight pushing through the Creator's pea soup fog, silhouetting man's majestic architecture.

Our lives are God's art. *For we are his workmanship, created in Christ Jesus for good works, which God prepared beforehand, that we should walk in them.*[3] When we are standing in the shatter of sorrow, dreams unfulfilled, blind fear, accidents, and death, we may only see chaos in the scattered pieces. For some, the Master gives space and time to back up, to look again with eyes trained by deeper encounters with life. Then comes illumination. The light of wisdom gained by seeking the King of Kings gives us peace. By His grace, we find beauty, at least in the sense of things, where once we saw only slivers and splinters and shards.

Like the shadowy earth, poised on the brink of dawn each morning, we long for the Creator's presence in our lives. Cracking through our darkness, comes the Light of the World, the risen Christ, who promises his faithful a resurrection. We yearn for His Spirit. We need His Light through our broken pieces. In His Kingdom, all in us that is broken will be made new. In such confidence, I live.

Gloria Dei!

End Notes

End Notes

Chapter 1. Child of Storms

1. https://time.com/5696288/hurricane-names

2. Nina Renata Aron, "The Terrifying History of 'Twilight Sleep,'" Jan. 17, 2018 https://timeline.com-restraints

Chapter 3. Raging September Sisters

1. Hurricane Donna. https://www.sun-sentinel.com/news/sfl-1960-hurricane-story.html.

Chapter 5. Too Late to Escape

1. 1 Corinthians 13:12

Chapter 6. Weather Behind Walls

1. https://www.washingtonpost.com/national/robert-simpson-co-creator-of-1-to-5-hurricane-model-dies-at-102/2014/12/20/3ecfa5ce-87b0-11e4-a702-fa31ff4ae98e story.html (accessed June 30, 2021)

Chapter 11. Bring Boots and a Helmet

1. Matthew 6:19-21

Chapter 12. Thunder in the Tropics

1. Phonophobia. https://www.verywellmind.com/
   fear-of-loud-noises-2671882

Chapter 14. Does a Home Have a Soul?

1. Luke 12:32-34

Chapter 17. Encountering Splendor and Grief

1. Natalie Goldberg, *Writing Down the Bones*
   (Boston, MA: Shambhala Publications, 1986), 9.

Chapter 19. Roads Back to Grit and Ghosts

1. Christie Purifoy, *Placemaker* (Grand Rapids,
   MI: Zondervan, 2019), 214.

2. Henri J. M. Nouwen, *The Way of the Heart*
   (New York, NY: Ballantine Books, 2003),
   17-18.

Chapter 20. Groans Too Deep for Words

1. Romans 8:26

Chapter 21. On My Knees Behind the Wheel

1. Brennan Manning, *The Ragamuffin Gospel*
   (Colorado Springs, CO: Multnomah Books,
   1990, 2000, 2005), 40.

Chapter 22. Answering the Call

1. Psalm 139:13
2. John 11:32-44
3. John 3:16
4. Isaiah 55:8

Chapter 23. Refined and Re-defined

1. Thomas Wolfe, *You Can't Go Home Again* (New York, London: Harper Row, 1940).
2. Kris Camealy, *Everything is Yours* (Refine Media, 2019) 104.

Chapter 24. Where was Our Son?

1. Luke 2:46-51

Chapter 26. A Few Farewells and Last Flight Out

1. John 15:13

Chapter 27. Pecans, Praise, and Prison

1. Luke 24:13-17; 30-31
2. Matthew 28:16-20

Chapter 28. Soft Songs and a Child's Psalm

1. Will L. Thompson. "Softly and Tenderly." Public Domain. 1880.
2. Psalm 23:1,6

Chapter 29. A Risk in the Spotlight

1. Matthew 18:21-22 NKJV

2. Romans 12:4-7

3. 1 Corinthians 12:27-28

4. Titus 2:7-8

5. John 8:12

Chapter 30. Fear Not Shore Birds

1. Luke 12:6-7

2. Frederick Buechner, Beyond Words: Daily Readings in the ABC's of Faith (Harper Collins, NY 2004), Quote 1024

3. Psalm 127:1

4. Romans 8:28

5. Joshua 24:15

Epilogue

1. Psalm 23:3

2. Corrie Ten Boom and Elizabeth and John Sherrill, *The Hiding Place* (Grand Rapids, MI: Chosen Books,1971), 234.

3. Ephesians 2:10

Also by This Author

SOFT TRADES, HARD BLOWS

A Poetry Collection

Available at Amazon Books

Made in the USA
Columbia, SC
24 October 2021

47523418R00171